Edward D. Andrews

REASONABLE FAITH

Saving Those Who Doubt

REASONABLE FAITH

Saving Those Who Doubt

"but in your hearts honor Christ the Lord as holy, always being prepared to make a defense to anyone who asks you for a reason for the hope that is in you" - 1 Peter 3:15

Edward D. Andrews

Christian Publishing House

Cambridge, Ohio

Copyright © 2018 Edward D. Andrews

All rights reserved. Except for brief quotations in articles, other publications, book reviews, and blogs, no part of this book may be reproduced in any manner without prior written permission from the publishers. For information, write,

support@christianpublishers.org

REASONABLE FAITH: Saving Those Who Doubt by Edward D. Andrews

- **ISBN-10** : 1945757914
- **ISBN-13** : 978-1945757914

Table of Contents

PREFACE 7
INTRODUCTION 9
Chapter 1 – The Nature of Doubt 11
Chapter 2 – The Foundation of Faith 18
Chapter 3 – The Authority of Scripture............................ 25
Chapter 4 – Jesus Christ: The Anchor of Belief 32
Chapter 5 – The Problem of Evil and Suffering 39
Chapter 6 – The Witness of Creation................................ 46
Chapter 7 – The Reliability of the Gospels 53
Chapter 8 – The Reality of the Resurrection 60
Chapter 9 – Faith and the Mind.. 67
Chapter 10 – The Role of the Holy Spirit 74
Chapter 11 – Overcoming Intellectual Barriers............... 82
Chapter 12 – The Assurance of Salvation........................ 90
Chapter 13 – The Church and the Defense of Faith 96
Chapter 14 – Faith in a Postmodern World 103
Chapter 15 – Science and Scripture................................. 110
Chapter 16 – When God Seems Silent............................. 117
Chapter 17 – The Discipline of Faith............................... 124
Chapter 18 – The Power of Testimony 131
Chapter 19 – Faith That Endures..................................... 137
Chapter 20 – The Ultimate Reward of Faith 145
Appendix A – Strengthening the Doubter 151

Appendix B – How Can We No Longer Walk in the Futility of the Old Mind?... 158

Appendix C – How Can We Deal with Spiritual Sicknesses of Mind and Heart?.. 166

Bibliography 173

PREFACE

Faith has always required reasoned conviction—not blind sentiment, not emotional fervor, but informed trust grounded in divine revelation. This volume, *Reasonable Faith: Saving Those Who Doubt*, was written to meet one of the most pressing needs within the Church today: the restoration of confidence in the reliability of Scripture, the reality of Christ, and the rational foundation of belief.

Modern Christianity often suffers from two extremes—emotional enthusiasm divorced from doctrine and intellectual skepticism detached from devotion. Both lead to spiritual instability. The purpose of this work is to reestablish the harmony between faith and reason as presented in Scripture itself. The apostolic command is clear: *"Always be ready to make a defense to everyone who asks you to give an account for the hope that is in you"* (1 Peter 3:15). That defense is not a weapon of pride but a ministry of mercy to those who waver, that they may find strength, assurance, and peace in the truth of God's Word.

This book proceeds from the conviction that doubt, though perilous if left unchecked, can become a catalyst for deeper conviction when confronted with Scripture and sound reasoning. Jehovah invites His people to *"reason together"* (Isaiah 1:18). The Christian, therefore, is called not to suppress inquiry but to bring every question into the light of divine revelation. When faith is examined through the lens of the Word, it is not diminished but refined.

Each chapter builds systematically upon the last—from the nature of doubt, to the foundation and authority of faith, to the evidences that confirm the Christian message. The objective is not mere apologetic argumentation but the cultivation of unwavering confidence in Jehovah's truth. Whether confronting intellectual challenges, moral confusion, or emotional struggle, the believer will find in these pages a framework for steadfast trust and rational devotion.

It is my earnest prayer that this work will equip pastors, teachers, and all sincere seekers of truth to stand firm in an age of uncertainty. May it help strengthen the weak, encourage the doubting, and call every reader to the maturity of a faith that both thinks deeply and believes completely.

Edward D. Andrews

Author of 220 books and Chief Translator of the Updated American Standard Version

INTRODUCTION

Faith does not thrive in ignorance but in understanding. The Christian's confidence in Jehovah must rest upon truth revealed through Scripture, verified by history, and confirmed through reasoned conviction. In an age where skepticism is exalted as intellectual virtue and biblical faith is dismissed as naïve, the need for a reasonable and steadfast faith has never been greater.

This book is written for those who struggle to believe, not because they love sin, but because they wrestle with uncertainty. Many within the church suffer silently under the weight of unanswered questions, fearing that doubt disqualifies them from true discipleship. Yet Scripture portrays doubt not as unforgivable weakness, but as an opportunity for growth. The man who cried, *"I do believe; help my unbelief"* (Mark 9:24), was not rejected by Christ but strengthened by Him. Jehovah's Word provides the light necessary to transform confusion into conviction and wavering into worship.

The purpose of *Reasonable Faith* is to guide the reader through that process of transformation. It seeks to bridge the gulf between belief and reason, showing that faith is not the abandonment of intellect but its highest expression under divine revelation. Faith is reasonable because it is grounded in the Word of the living God, Who cannot lie. The Bible does not ask the believer to close his eyes to evidence but to interpret evidence through the lens of divine truth.

Each chapter builds upon the last, forming a systematic defense and cultivation of faith: beginning with the nature of doubt, moving through the authority of Scripture, the reality of Jesus Christ, and the evidences that validate the gospel message. The later sections address the endurance of faith in suffering, the harmony between science and

Scripture, and the ultimate hope that sustains believers until Christ's return. Throughout, the emphasis remains on the sufficiency of God's Word as the only sure foundation for belief and the only effective remedy for doubt.

Reasonable faith does not rest upon emotional experience or ecclesiastical tradition but upon the inspired Word of Jehovah and the verifiable testimony of history. Christianity invites examination because it is grounded in reality, not speculation. The resurrection of Jesus Christ, the preservation of Scripture, and the testimony of creation all stand as enduring witnesses to truth that reason can affirm and faith can embrace.

The reader is therefore invited to approach this work not merely as an academic study but as a spiritual journey. The aim is not only to defend the faith but to deepen it—to move from uncertainty to conviction, from mere assent to living trust. May those who read with an open Bible and a receptive heart find that faith in Jehovah is both intellectually sound and spiritually unshakable.

Chapter 1 – The Nature of Doubt

Main Verse: Jude 22 – "And have mercy on those who doubt."

Doubt has long occupied a critical place in the Christian journey, being both a reflection of human limitation and a point of potential spiritual growth. Jude, in his brief yet profound epistle, addresses the believer's responsibility toward those who waver, commanding mercy rather than condemnation. This verse strikes at the very heart of Christian compassion and discernment, reminding us that those struggling with uncertainty must not be crushed under judgment but uplifted with understanding. True faith does not fear examination, for it is founded upon truth revealed by Jehovah through His Word. To understand the nature of doubt, one must distinguish between questioning and unbelief, explore the human condition that gives rise to weak faith, discern Satan's influence in exploiting uncertainty, recognize God's gracious invitation to honest inquiry, appreciate the conscience's role in spiritual formation, and finally, see doubt as a means for achieving deeper conviction.

Understanding the Difference Between Questioning and Unbelief

Questioning is not synonymous with unbelief. Questioning arises from a sincere desire to understand, whereas unbelief results from a willful rejection of truth. Throughout Scripture, Jehovah demonstrates patience with those who question out of humility. For instance, Mary asked the angel Gabriel, "How will this be, since I am a virgin?" (Luke 1:34). Her question did not spring from defiance but from honest wonder and a yearning to comprehend God's method. In contrast, Zechariah's question, "How can I be sure of this?" (Luke 1:18), carried an undertone of skepticism, implying doubt in the reliability of God's promise. The former was met with reassurance, the latter with discipline. Thus, the distinction lies in the heart's posture toward God.

Unbelief, by contrast, is the hardened state of resisting God's revelation. It is not ignorance or confusion but rebellion. The Israelites in the wilderness exemplified unbelief; they saw Jehovah's mighty acts yet hardened their hearts (Hebrews 3:7–19). Unbelief is not the product of inadequate evidence but of a defiant will that refuses to trust. When Jesus appeared after His resurrection, Thomas's initial doubt gave way to worship once confronted with truth (John 20:24–28). His questioning was not unbelief, for once presented with evidence, he surrendered in faith. Thus, questioning becomes the soil in which genuine conviction may grow, but unbelief is the rocky ground that refuses cultivation.

The Human Condition and the Reality of Weak Faith

Faith, though divinely anchored, operates within the frailty of human nature. Because humanity is imperfect, even sincere believers wrestle with moments of weakness. The father who cried out to Jesus, "I do believe; help my unbelief!" (Mark 9:24), expressed the tension between faith and doubt that resides in every believer's heart. Jehovah does not reject such weakness; rather, He works within it, perfecting faith through dependence on His Word.

Weak faith arises from spiritual immaturity, limited understanding, or emotional turmoil. Circumstances such as loss, disappointment, or prolonged suffering may shake one's assurance in God's promises. Yet, Jehovah's compassion meets us in our frailty. The Psalms repeatedly capture this human vulnerability. David often poured out his soul in confusion, questioning why God seemed distant or why the wicked prospered (Psalm 13:1–2; 73:2–3). However, these laments did not culminate in rebellion but in renewed trust. True faith is not the absence of doubt but the decision to cling to Jehovah despite uncertainty.

Weak faith is not fatal faith. Just as a flickering flame can be fanned into brightness, so wavering belief can mature through divine patience and biblical instruction. Jesus described faith as a mustard seed (Matthew 17:20), emphasizing that its size matters less than its presence and direction. Even the smallest faith, rightly placed in Jehovah, contains boundless potential for growth.

Satan's Role in Exploiting Uncertainty

Satan's most effective weapon against believers is the distortion of truth through doubt. From the beginning, his strategy has been to twist Jehovah's words. In Eden, he asked Eve, "Did God really say…?"

(Genesis 3:1), planting suspicion toward divine goodness. That same tactic continues today. The Adversary knows that open rebellion may repel the faithful, but subtle doubt erodes trust gradually.

Satan exploits emotional vulnerability, intellectual pride, and spiritual fatigue. He whispers that God's promises are unreliable, that prayer is futile, or that Scripture cannot be trusted. The aim is not to provoke inquiry but to sever confidence in Jehovah's authority. His objective is unbelief masked as intellectual honesty. Paul warned that Satan masquerades as an angel of light (2 Corinthians 11:14), appealing to the mind's desire for autonomy rather than submission to divine revelation.

Believers must therefore guard their minds by renewing them with Scripture (Romans 12:2). Doubt becomes destructive when detached from the corrective influence of God's Word. Without the anchor of truth, uncertainty drifts into cynicism, and curiosity becomes rebellion. Satan capitalizes on that drift, urging believers to rely on human wisdom rather than divine revelation. Recognizing his role in exploiting doubt equips Christians to respond not with despair but with vigilance.

God's Invitation to Honest Inquiry

Jehovah does not silence inquiry; He welcomes it when it springs from a sincere heart. The Scriptures repeatedly invite reasoning and examination. Isaiah 1:18 records Jehovah's appeal, "Come now, let us reason together." This is not the invitation of a tyrant demanding blind allegiance but of a loving Creator appealing to rational creatures made in His image. Faith and reason are not adversaries but allies under divine truth.

The Bereans exemplify this balanced approach. They "examined the Scriptures daily to see if these things were so" (Acts 17:11). Their examination was not rooted in suspicion but in discernment. They believed because the evidence confirmed the message. Similarly, Jesus Himself did not condemn John the Baptist when he sent messengers to ask, "Are You the One who is to come?" (Matthew 11:3). Instead, Jesus pointed to His works as verification, strengthening John's faith through evidence.

Honest inquiry leads to mature conviction because it tests beliefs against divine revelation. The Spirit-inspired Word contains the answers necessary for sound doctrine and spiritual assurance. Jehovah does not fear scrutiny, for His truth is absolute and self-consistent. The believer, therefore, need not suppress questions but must bring them into the light of Scripture where error is exposed and faith fortified.

The Role of the Conscience in Faith Formation

The conscience, as designed by Jehovah, serves as an internal moral compass. However, because of sin, it is not infallible and requires calibration through God's Word. When the conscience is trained by truth, it becomes a vital ally in faith formation. It alerts the believer to spiritual inconsistency and convicts the heart when faith wavers.

A seared conscience, on the other hand, loses sensitivity to truth, paving the way for rationalized doubt and moral compromise (1 Timothy 4:2). When the conscience is neglected, faith becomes hollow ritual rather than heartfelt devotion. Yet, when properly instructed, the conscience helps maintain integrity before Jehovah, ensuring that faith remains both sincere and obedient.

Paul's testimony illustrates this balance: "I always strive to keep my conscience clear before God and man" (Acts 24:16). A clear conscience does not mean freedom from doubt but freedom from hypocrisy. It means aligning belief and behavior so that faith operates in both conviction and conduct. As the believer meditates on Scripture, the conscience becomes strengthened, resisting Satan's deceptions and preserving confidence in Jehovah's promises.

Doubt as an Opportunity for Deeper Conviction

Though doubt can be perilous if left unchecked, it also presents an opportunity for growth. Jehovah often allows believers to experience moments of uncertainty to drive them toward deeper understanding and dependence on Him. Spiritual maturity is forged through the process of wrestling with questions in the presence of God.

The disciples themselves were not immune to doubt. When Peter walked on the water, fear overtook faith, and he began to sink. Jesus said, "You of little faith, why did you doubt?" (Matthew 14:31). Yet from this event, Peter learned the necessity of fixing his eyes on Christ. His later boldness in Acts reveals how past uncertainty became a platform for unwavering conviction. Jehovah refines faith not by removing all questions but by anchoring the heart more securely in truth.

The process of overcoming doubt strengthens humility, dependence, and discernment. Each time a believer resolves uncertainty through Scripture and prayer, faith becomes more resilient. Doubt, when surrendered to God, becomes a stepping stone toward steadfast conviction. As Jude instructs, mercy must govern our approach to those who waver, for their struggle may become the very means by which Jehovah perfects their trust.

REASONABLE FAITH

In the end, doubt does not define the believer's identity—faith does. The Christian who perseveres through questioning, resists Satan's deceit, and seeks truth in Jehovah's Word emerges with a fortified belief capable of withstanding opposition. Therefore, doubt, rather than being the enemy of faith, becomes its refining instrument when met with humility, Scripture, and divine mercy.

Chapter 2 – The Foundation of Faith

Main Verse: Hebrews 11:1 – "Now faith is the assurance of things hoped for, the conviction of things not seen."

Faith lies at the very core of the Christian life. It is the divine bridge that connects finite humanity with the infinite God, forming the essential means by which salvation, obedience, and endurance are made possible. The inspired writer of Hebrews defines faith not as wishful thinking or blind optimism but as solid assurance and firm conviction rooted in Jehovah's revealed Word. Faith is both rational and relational—rational because it is based upon verifiable truth, and relational because it involves personal trust in the unchanging character of Jehovah. The Christian's faith is not born of emotion or imagination but grounded in the living testimony of Scripture and confirmed by the Spirit's witness through that Word.

The Biblical Definition of Faith

Hebrews 11:1 provides the definitive biblical definition of faith: "Now faith is the assurance of things hoped for, the conviction of things not seen." The Greek term translated "assurance" (hypostasis) denotes a firm foundation, a confidence or substantial reality. It conveys that faith is not a mere mental assent but a tangible certainty regarding the promises of God. The word rendered "conviction" (elegchos) carries the idea of evidence or proof, referring to the inner certainty produced by trusting God's revelation. Faith, therefore, is not belief without evidence but confidence grounded in divine evidence—Jehovah's Word itself.

Faith operates within the realm of unseen realities. The believer does not see the full fulfillment of God's promises in the present, yet possesses an unshakable assurance that they are true. This assurance is not grounded in human perception but in the reliability of God's Word. The same chapter of Hebrews illustrates this through the lives of Abel, Enoch, Noah, Abraham, and others who acted upon divine truth without possessing complete sight of its outcome. Their obedience testified that faith is not passive assent but active trust.

The biblical concept of faith encompasses three components: knowledge, assent, and trust. Knowledge involves understanding what God has revealed. Assent signifies agreement that what He has spoken is true. Trust, the heart of saving faith, is personal reliance upon Jehovah's promises through Christ. Without this trust, faith remains intellectual but not transformative. Thus, faith is both objective—resting upon divine revelation—and subjective—transforming the inner person through that truth.

The Relationship Between Faith and Reason

Faith and reason are not enemies but allies when rightly understood. Genuine faith never contradicts sound reason; rather, it transcends reason by resting upon revelation that reason alone could never discover. Reason allows us to analyze and comprehend; faith enables us to accept and apply. The apostle Paul appealed to reason when he said, "I know whom I have believed" (2 Timothy 1:12). He did not believe blindly but rationally, based on evidence and personal experience of God's faithfulness.

Jehovah invites rational faith. Isaiah 1:18 records His appeal, "Come now, let us reason together." This invitation affirms that faith is not irrational submission but reason enlightened by divine truth. While human reason can recognize the necessity of a Creator, only revelation unveils His nature, will, and redemptive purpose. Thus, faith completes what reason begins.

Faith without reason becomes fanaticism; reason without faith becomes skepticism. The balance between the two ensures stability. The believer uses reason to understand the facts of Scripture and faith to trust their reliability and live by them. Abraham reasoned that God could raise Isaac from the dead (Hebrews 11:19); his faith was informed, not blind. True biblical faith stands upon historical fact, prophetic fulfillment, and divine consistency. The harmony of faith and reason demonstrates that Christianity rests upon objective truth rather than emotional or mystical experience.

Faith as Trust in the Character of Jehovah

At its core, faith is not merely belief in doctrines but trust in the Person of Jehovah. The Christian does not place faith in faith itself but in the One who is utterly trustworthy. Jehovah's character—His holiness, justice, wisdom, and love—forms the unshakable foundation of faith. Scripture repeatedly emphasizes this aspect. The psalmist declares, "Those who know Your name will trust in You, for You, Jehovah, have never forsaken those who seek You" (Psalm 9:10).

To trust Jehovah's character means to rely upon His promises even when circumstances appear contrary. Abraham's faith exemplifies this principle. Though his body was "as good as dead" and Sarah's womb barren, he did not waver in unbelief but was "fully convinced that God was able to do what He had promised" (Romans 4:19–21). His faith was not optimism about his situation but confidence in the integrity of God's nature.

Faith in Jehovah's character also includes submission to His timing and wisdom. It requires the believer to acknowledge that God's ways are higher than human comprehension (Isaiah 55:8–9). This trust does not negate human responsibility but harmonizes with obedience. The believer's assurance rests not in personal understanding but in the constancy of Jehovah's truthfulness. Faith grows as one studies His Word, observes His faithfulness, and experiences His providential care.

Faith Anchored in Revelation, Not Emotion

Modern culture often equates faith with feeling, but biblical faith is not dependent on emotional experience. Emotion may accompany faith, but it does not define or sustain it. Faith anchored in feelings will falter when emotions shift, but faith rooted in revelation remains steadfast. Jehovah's Word provides objective truth that transcends human sentiment.

The prophet Habakkuk, facing confusion and fear, declared, "The righteous will live by faith" (Habakkuk 2:4). His confidence was not in circumstances but in God's promises. Likewise, Jesus reminded His disciples that faith must rest upon His words, not transient impressions. "Heaven and earth will pass away, but my words will never pass away" (Matthew 24:35). Faith must therefore be anchored in the immovable authority of Scripture.

The believer must learn to distinguish between spiritual assurance and emotional comfort. Feelings may affirm faith, but they cannot establish it. The anchor of the soul, as Hebrews 6:19 describes, is hope fixed in the promises of God, not the fluctuations of emotion. Genuine faith persists through hardship, even when spiritual joy seems absent, because it rests on the certainty of Jehovah's revelation.

The Witness of the Spirit Through the Word

The Spirit bears witness to faith, not through mystical impressions but through the objective testimony of Scripture. Jesus declared, "The words that I have spoken to you are spirit and life" (John 6:63). The Spirit's operation today is through the inspired Word He authored, illuminating its meaning and strengthening believers to apply it.

Romans 10:17 teaches, "Faith comes from hearing, and hearing through the word of Christ." This verse identifies Scripture as the exclusive channel through which faith is generated and sustained. The Spirit does not implant faith apart from the Word but works within it, bringing conviction and clarity. This explains why the apostles continually preached and taught from the Scriptures, knowing that divine truth produces faith in receptive hearts.

The Spirit's witness through the Word assures believers of their relationship with Jehovah. "The Spirit Himself bears witness with our spirit that we are children of God" (Romans 8:16). This witness is not an emotional sensation but the alignment of one's life with Scripture's testimony. As the believer obeys the Word, the Spirit affirms assurance by confirming that such obedience reflects genuine faith. Faith is strengthened when it is exercised in conformity with divine revelation, not through mystical encounters or subjective impressions.

Building Confidence Through Scripture

Faith matures through continual engagement with Scripture. The believer builds confidence not by striving for emotional certainty but by deepening understanding of Jehovah's truth. The Psalmist wrote, "The law of Jehovah is perfect, restoring the soul; the testimony of Jehovah is sure, making wise the simple" (Psalm 19:7). The more one studies and meditates upon God's Word, the more faith becomes robust, rational, and enduring.

Faith grows as knowledge of God increases. Peter exhorted believers to "grow in the grace and knowledge of our Lord and Savior Jesus Christ" (2 Peter 3:18). Knowledge does not replace faith but nourishes it, providing the foundation upon which assurance rests. Every promise, prophecy, and precept in Scripture serves to fortify trust in Jehovah's reliability.

The believer's confidence is built through remembering past evidences of God's faithfulness. The patriarchs trusted Jehovah because they had witnessed His power and truth. Modern Christians share in that same legacy, possessing the complete revelation of God's Word as a sure testimony. The more we immerse ourselves in Scripture, the less vulnerable we become to doubt or deception.

Faith's strength is not measured by intensity of emotion but by constancy of conviction. The mature believer learns to trust Jehovah even in silence, knowing that His Word endures forever. When faith is founded upon divine revelation, it remains unshaken by circumstance. Thus, the foundation of faith is not built upon the shifting sands of human feeling or speculation but upon the unchanging Rock of Jehovah's truth revealed through Scripture.

Chapter 3 – The Authority of Scripture

Main Verse: 2 Timothy 3:16 – "All Scripture is inspired by God and profitable for teaching, for reproof, for correction, for training in righteousness."

The authority of Scripture stands as the cornerstone of Christian faith, defining the believer's understanding of truth, morality, salvation, and the nature of God Himself. In 2 Timothy 3:16, the apostle Paul establishes the foundation of biblical authority by affirming that "All Scripture is inspired by God." The phrase literally means "God-breathed" (Greek: *theopneustos*), indicating that the very words of the Bible originated from Jehovah through the direct operation of His Spirit. Scripture, therefore, is not the product of human invention but of divine revelation communicated through human instruments. Its authority is absolute, final, and binding upon every believer. To understand this fully, we must consider the divine inspiration of the Bible, its historical reliability, the confirming power of prophecy, the way Scripture equips the believer, its superiority over human philosophy, and the rational defense of its inerrancy.

The Divine Inspiration of the Bible

The Bible claims inspiration not merely in concept but in word. Inspiration means that Jehovah superintended the human authors so that, while using their individual vocabulary, style, and cultural context, they wrote exactly what He intended, free from error in the original autographs. Peter confirms this when he writes, "Men spoke from God as they were carried along by the Holy Spirit" (2 Peter 1:21). The verb *pherō* ("carried along") conveys the image of a ship driven by the wind. The human authors did not drift under their own momentum but were moved and directed by the Spirit's power.

This inspiration extended to every part of Scripture—its history, doctrine, prophecy, and moral instruction. Jesus Himself affirmed verbal inspiration when He declared, "Scripture cannot be broken" (John 10:35) and when He said that not even "one jot or one tittle" would pass from the Law until all was fulfilled (Matthew 5:18). Every word bears divine authority because every word is God-breathed.

While Jehovah did not miraculously preserve the physical manuscripts, He has preserved and restored His Word through faithful textual transmission and restoration. Through the meticulous copying practices of the Hebrew scribes, the early Christian scribes, and the thousands of extant manuscripts, modern textual scholarship has restored the biblical text to 99.99% accuracy with the inspired originals. The Bible we possess today, derived from the Hebrew and Greek critical texts, faithfully represents the inspired writings. Thus, inspiration belongs to the original autographs, and preservation exists through the providential restoration of the text across history.

The Historical Reliability of the Text

The authority of Scripture is not an abstract claim but one supported by historical reliability. The Bible's textual, archaeological, and historical integrity establishes it as the most trustworthy ancient record in existence.

Textually, the manuscript evidence for both the Old and New Testaments is unparalleled. The discovery of the Dead Sea Scrolls confirmed that the Hebrew text of Isaiah, copied over a thousand years earlier than any previously known manuscripts, was virtually identical to later versions. This demonstrates the precision of textual transmission and the reliability of restoration. Similarly, over 5,800 Greek manuscripts of the New Testament exist, along with thousands of early translations and quotations from the Church Fathers that allow scholars to reconstruct the original wording with remarkable accuracy.

Historically, the events recorded in Scripture correspond with verified archaeological findings. Excavations at Jericho, Hazor, Nineveh, and Babylon have provided evidence consistent with biblical accounts. Ancient inscriptions have confirmed the existence of figures such as David, Hezekiah, and Pontius Pilate. The historical framework of Scripture is therefore not mythic or symbolic but factual and verifiable.

The reliability of the biblical text affirms its authority because a corrupted or uncertain text could not serve as a divine standard. Yet Jehovah, in His wisdom, ensured that His revelation was accurately transmitted and restored for all generations. Faith in the Bible's authority, therefore, rests upon verifiable historical evidence and divine integrity rather than blind tradition.

The Role of Prophecy in Confirming Truth

Prophecy functions as Jehovah's irrefutable proof of Scripture's divine origin. Through prophecy, God reveals His omniscience and sovereignty over time and history. No other book in the world has foretold the future with such accuracy and fulfillment as the Bible.

Isaiah prophesied the rise of Cyrus by name nearly two centuries before his birth (Isaiah 44:28–45:1), and Daniel outlined the succession of empires from Babylon to Rome (Daniel 2, 7, 8). Most compelling of all are the messianic prophecies fulfilled in Jesus Christ—His virgin birth (Isaiah 7:14), His ministry in Galilee (Isaiah 9:1–2), His atoning death (Isaiah 53), and His resurrection (Psalm 16:10). The statistical probability of these prophecies being fulfilled by chance is astronomically low, demonstrating that the Bible is not a product of human foresight but of divine revelation.

Prophecy also affirms the continuing relevance of Scripture. It reminds believers that Jehovah's Word does not merely record the past but governs the future. Peter wrote that "we have the prophetic word more fully confirmed" (2 Peter 1:19), emphasizing that fulfilled prophecy strengthens faith and confirms the authority of the entire biblical message.

How the Scriptures Equip the Believer

Paul declared that Scripture is "profitable for teaching, for reproof, for correction, for training in righteousness" (2 Timothy 3:16). Each of these functions reveals the authority and sufficiency of the Word.

Teaching refers to doctrinal instruction—Scripture establishes truth and defines what must be believed. Reproof exposes error, confronting false teaching and sinful conduct. Correction restores believers to right living by aligning their thoughts and actions with God's standards. Training in righteousness shapes the character and conduct of those who seek to live godly lives in an ungodly world. The Word of God, therefore, is not static information but living instruction that transforms the believer from within.

Paul continues, "that the man of God may be complete, equipped for every good work" (2 Timothy 3:17). This completeness (*artios*) signifies full spiritual maturity, a readiness to meet the demands of Christian service. Scripture alone can produce this maturity, for it contains everything necessary for faith and godliness. No other source—human philosophy, church tradition, or mystical experience—can equip the believer as Scripture does. The authority of the Bible lies not only in its origin but in its transformative power.

The Bible Versus Human Philosophy

Human philosophy, while sometimes insightful in natural matters, cannot serve as a foundation for truth or morality. Paul warns, "See to it that no one takes you captive through philosophy and empty deception, according to human tradition, according to the elementary principles of the world, rather than according to Christ" (Colossians 2:8). Human reasoning, detached from revelation, is finite and flawed. Philosophy begins with man's ideas about reality; Scripture begins with God's revelation of reality.

Throughout history, human philosophy has shifted like sand—ancient Greek rationalism, Enlightenment skepticism, existentialism, and modern relativism have all sought to redefine truth apart from God. Yet each system collapses under its own inconsistency. Only Scripture provides an unchanging standard for truth, morality, and meaning because it proceeds from Jehovah, who is Himself unchanging (Malachi 3:6).

The authority of Scripture exposes the limitations of human thought. While reason and logic have their place, they must operate under the supremacy of revelation. Faith seeks understanding, but understanding must be guided by faith in the God-breathed Word. To build life upon human philosophy is to construct upon shifting sand; to build upon Scripture is to stand upon the Rock that cannot be moved.

Defending the Inerrancy of the Word

Inerrancy means that the Scriptures, in their original autographs, are completely without error in all they affirm—whether spiritual, historical, or moral. The inerrancy of Scripture follows logically from its divine inspiration: if God is perfect, His Word must also be perfect. "The words of Jehovah are pure words, like silver refined in a furnace on the ground, purified seven times" (Psalm 12:6).

The charge of error in Scripture arises not from the text but from misinterpretation, inadequate translation, or ignorance of historical and linguistic context. When properly understood, the Bible has proven accurate in every field it touches—history, geography, and moral instruction. The restoration of the text through critical scholarship has clarified rather than diminished its accuracy, confirming that any textual variations do not affect doctrine or essential truth.

Defending inerrancy is not a matter of intellectual pride but of reverence for God's authority. If Scripture contains error, its authority collapses; if it is wholly true, it commands full submission. Jesus Himself affirmed the inerrancy of the Old Testament when He said, "Your word is truth" (John 17:17). The believer's confidence in the Bible's authority rests upon this same conviction.

The authority of Scripture, therefore, stands firm upon the combined witness of inspiration, reliability, prophecy, transformative power, and inerrancy. It is Jehovah's final revelation to humanity, the unchanging standard against which all ideas, actions, and beliefs must be measured. To reject its authority is to reject the voice of God Himself. To submit to it is to build one's life upon unshakable truth.

Chapter 4 – Jesus Christ: The Anchor of Belief

Main Verse: John 14:6 – "Jesus said to him, 'I am the way, and the truth, and the life; no one comes to the Father except through me.'"

At the heart of Christian faith stands the Person and work of Jesus Christ. In Him, every doctrine, every prophecy, and every hope of redemption converges. Without Christ, Christianity collapses into mere moralism or abstract philosophy; with Him, it becomes the revelation of God's plan for humanity. When Jesus declared, "I am the way, and the truth, and the life," He did not offer one path among many but the exclusive means of reconciliation with Jehovah. Every claim of Christianity—its authority, truthfulness, and power—rests upon who Jesus is and what He accomplished. He is not a mere historical figure or ethical teacher; He is the incarnate Son of God, the Redeemer, the risen Lord, and the eternal foundation of all belief.

To understand why Jesus Christ is the anchor of faith, we must consider the historical reliability of His life and works, the divine nature of His person, His moral perfection, the necessity of His atoning death, the certainty of His resurrection, and the present reality of His reign.

The Historical Jesus and the Testimony of Eyewitnesses

Faith in Jesus Christ is not blind sentiment but trust grounded in verifiable history. The New Testament presents Him not as a mythic creation but as a living, historical figure whose life was attested by numerous eyewitnesses. Luke affirms that his Gospel was compiled from firsthand testimony: "Just as those who from the beginning were eyewitnesses and servants of the word have handed them down to us" (Luke 1:2). The apostles did not follow "cleverly devised myths" but proclaimed what they had seen and heard (2 Peter 1:16).

The Gospel accounts bear the marks of historical authenticity. They include specific names, places, cultural details, and sequences of events that align with the archaeological and historical record. Pilate's governorship, Herod's rule, the customs of Jewish worship, and the geography of Galilee and Judea all corroborate the New Testament's reliability. The writings of early non-Christian historians, such as Josephus and Tacitus, also affirm that Jesus lived, was crucified under Pontius Pilate, and inspired a movement that continued after His death.

The eyewitness nature of the New Testament cannot be overstated. John writes, "That which we have seen with our eyes, which we have looked at and our hands have touched—this we proclaim" (1 John 1:1). The apostles' willingness to suffer and die for their testimony confirms their sincerity. Men may die for what they believe to be true, but not for what they know to be false. Thus, the foundation of Christian belief is historical reality confirmed by faithful witnesses, not religious imagination.

The Deity of Christ and Its Implications for Faith

Jesus Christ is not merely a moral reformer or inspired prophet—He is Jehovah's Son, fully divine and fully human. The Scriptures consistently affirm His deity. John declares, "In the beginning was the Word, and the Word was with God, and the Word was God" (John 1:1). When Thomas encountered the risen Christ, he confessed, "My Lord and my God!" (John 20:28). Paul writes, "In Him all the fullness of deity dwells bodily" (Colossians 2:9).

The deity of Christ is essential because only God can provide the atonement necessary for sin's forgiveness. No created being, no prophet, and no angel could bear the infinite moral debt owed to a holy God. Christ's divine nature ensures the sufficiency of His sacrifice. Moreover, His deity guarantees the trustworthiness of His revelation. As the Son who shares the Father's nature, He reveals God perfectly: "He who has seen me has seen the Father" (John 14:9).

Faith in Christ's deity transforms belief into worship. To trust Jesus as Lord is to acknowledge Him as Creator, Judge, and Redeemer. The confession "Jesus is Lord" (Romans 10:9) was the earliest declaration of Christian faith, marking the believer's submission to His absolute authority. If Jesus is God, then His words carry divine command; if He is not, then the entire gospel collapses into deception. Thus, the deity of Christ stands at the center of all Christian doctrine and faith.

The Sinless Life and Moral Perfection of the Savior

The credibility of Christ's mission rests upon His moral perfection. The testimony of Scripture, both from His friends and His foes, affirms His sinlessness. Peter described Him as "a lamb without blemish or spot" (1 Peter 1:19) and testified that He "committed no sin, nor was deceit found in his mouth" (1 Peter 2:22). The writer of Hebrews declares that He was "tempted in every way, yet without sin" (Hebrews 4:15). Even Pilate, though complicit in His execution, admitted, "I find no fault in Him" (John 19:6).

Jesus' sinlessness was not a mere absence of wrongdoing but the positive presence of perfect righteousness. Every thought, word, and deed was in harmony with the will of His Father. He not only kept the Law but fulfilled it completely (Matthew 5:17). His obedience was voluntary, not coerced, and His moral purity reflected the divine nature within Him.

This perfection qualified Him to be the substitute for sinners. Only a sinless man could bear the penalty of sin for others. His perfect life thus forms the moral basis of redemption. The believer's faith is not in a flawed example but in a flawless Savior whose righteousness is imputed to all who trust in Him.

The Cross: A Rational and Moral Necessity

The cross of Christ is not an arbitrary or cruel event—it is the rational and moral necessity of divine justice. Sin cannot be overlooked; Jehovah's holiness demands that it be judged. Yet His love desires reconciliation. The cross resolves this tension perfectly. Paul explains, "He made him who knew no sin to be sin on our behalf, so that we might become the righteousness of God in him" (2 Corinthians 5:21).

The atonement is not divine injustice but divine substitution. The penalty of sin—death—was borne by the sinless Christ so that God could remain just while justifying the sinner who believes (Romans 3:26). Human wisdom cannot produce such a solution, for no philosophy or religion offers both absolute justice and absolute mercy without contradiction. Only the cross satisfies both.

Faith finds its anchor in the cross because there Jehovah's character is fully revealed. The believer does not hope in an undefined deity but in the God who entered human history, bore human sin, and accomplished eternal redemption. The cross is the central fact of Christian theology and the moral center of all history.

The Resurrection as the Cornerstone of Proof

The resurrection of Jesus Christ is the defining proof of His identity and the vindication of His claims. Without it, Christianity would be an empty philosophy; with it, faith stands upon unshakable evidence. Paul wrote, "If Christ has not been raised, your faith is worthless" (1 Corinthians 15:17). The resurrection is not an optional belief but the cornerstone of Christian hope.

The historical evidence for the resurrection is overwhelming. The tomb was empty, the body was never found, and numerous witnesses saw the risen Christ under varied circumstances. The disciples' transformation from fear to bold proclamation testifies to their certainty of His victory over death. The enemies of the gospel could have silenced it by producing the body, yet history records no such act.

Furthermore, the resurrection explains the rapid expansion of the early church. The apostles did not preach an idea but a living reality. Their message centered on a risen Savior who had conquered sin and death. This fact turned despair into faith and persecution into perseverance. The resurrection demonstrates that faith in Christ is not belief in an ideal but in a living Lord whose presence continues to sustain His people.

The Present Reign of Christ

Jesus Christ is not only the risen Savior but the reigning Lord. After His resurrection, He ascended to the Father's right hand, where He exercises authority over heaven and earth. Paul declares that God "seated Him at His right hand in the heavenly places, far above all rule and authority" (Ephesians 1:20–21). His reign is not symbolic but active, guiding history toward the fulfillment of Jehovah's redemptive plan.

Christ's reign is both present and future. Presently, He rules in the hearts of believers and through His spiritual kingdom, the church. He governs by His Word, intercedes as High Priest, and sustains His people through divine providence. Futurely, He will return to establish His Millennial Kingdom, ruling the earth in righteousness and peace (Revelation 20:4–6).

The believer's faith finds confidence in this ongoing reign. Jesus is not a memory of the past but the living Sovereign who upholds all things by the word of His power (Hebrews 1:3). His promises are certain because His authority is absolute. He remains the same yesterday, today, and forever (Hebrews 13:8).

Christ, therefore, is the immovable anchor of belief—the One in whom faith finds both its foundation and fulfillment. To believe in Him is not to embrace an abstract system but to entrust oneself to the living God who became man for our redemption. His historical reality, divine identity, moral perfection, sacrificial death, victorious resurrection, and reigning authority together form the unbreakable chain of truth that secures the believer's soul.

REASONABLE FAITH

Chapter 5 – The Problem of Evil and Suffering

Main Verse: Romans 8:28 – "And we know that God causes all things to work together for good to those who love God."

Few subjects challenge the human heart and mind as deeply as the problem of evil and suffering. From natural disasters to personal loss, from moral evil to disease, the question persists: If Jehovah is good, loving, and all-powerful, why does He permit suffering? Scripture offers a profound answer that upholds both God's righteousness and His purpose. Romans 8:28 is often cited as comfort, but it is frequently misunderstood. Paul was not claiming that every event in life is intrinsically good or that God directly orchestrates all outcomes. Instead, he declared that Jehovah, in His infinite wisdom, can cause all things—even the painful and unjust— to contribute toward ultimate good for those who love Him and remain loyal to His purpose. This assurance does not mean that God is the author of evil, but that He overrules it for redemptive ends.

Paul's Greek wording—*panta synergei eis agathon tois agapōsin ton theon*—literally means "all things are working together toward good for those who love God." The phrase *synergei* (from *synergeō*) conveys cooperation or joint action. It indicates not that each event individually is good, but that in God's sovereign plan, all events are coordinated to fulfill His purpose for the faithful. Thus, this verse reveals divine providence, not divine causation of suffering. Evil and suffering exist because of human rebellion and Satan's deceit, not because Jehovah ordains them. Yet God can use even the consequences of sin to accomplish ultimate spiritual good, refining character and fulfilling His redemptive plan in Christ.

To understand this more deeply, we must trace the origin of evil, the nature of free will, the limits of divine intervention, and the hope that Jesus and the Scriptures provide.

The Origin of Evil in Creation

Evil did not originate with Jehovah, for "His activity is perfect, for all his ways are justice" (Deuteronomy 32:4). The introduction of evil into creation arose through the misuse of free will by intelligent creatures—first by Satan, then by Adam and Eve. In the Garden of Eden, Jehovah had given humankind a simple command as a test of loyalty and love (Genesis 2:16–17). Adam and Eve disobeyed Jehovah and rebelled against Him, thinking that they could determine right and wrong independently. This was not a trivial error; it was a rejection of divine authority and an assertion of moral autonomy.

Jehovah could have immediately destroyed the rebels, but in His wisdom, He chose to allow time to vindicate His name and purpose. By granting mankind the freedom to rule themselves under Satan's influence, Jehovah permitted history to demonstrate conclusively that independence from Him leads to suffering, disorder, and death. Satan had charged that Jehovah's rule was unjust and that humans would serve God only for selfish reasons (Job 1:9–11). The divine response was to let time and human experience expose that lie.

Throughout the centuries, human governments, philosophies, and moral systems have failed to bring lasting peace or justice. The prophet Jeremiah accurately summarized this truth: "I well know, O Jehovah, that man's way does not belong to him. It does not belong to man who is walking even to direct his step" (Jeremiah 10:23). Jehovah has proven that His rule alone ensures righteousness, peace, and joy. Evil exists, therefore, not as a reflection of God's character but as a necessary stage in His plan to vindicate His sovereignty and demonstrate the moral necessity of obedience to Him.

How Was It Possible for Adam to Sin if He Was Perfect?

When Jehovah pronounced His creation "very good" (Genesis 1:31), it meant that all things were in complete harmony with His standards of perfection. Adam and Eve were flawless in body, mind, and spirit. However, moral perfection does not exclude the capacity to choose wrongly. To be perfect human beings, they had to possess freedom of choice; without it, they would have been mere automatons incapable of love or obedience born from genuine will.

Jehovah designed humans to choose right because they love Him, not because they are compelled to do so. Deuteronomy 30:19–20 presents this choice clearly: "I have put life and death before you, the blessing and the curse; and you must choose life so that you may keep alive, you and your offspring, by loving Jehovah your God." Love requires freedom, and freedom entails responsibility.

Adam and Eve's sin did not arise from a defect in their nature but from a failure of will. Eve entertained Satan's deception and allowed her desires to develop contrary to truth. Adam, though not deceived (1 Timothy 2:14), deliberately chose companionship with his wife over obedience to Jehovah. James 1:14–15 explains the moral process: "Each one is tried by being drawn out and enticed by his own desire. Then the desire, when it has become fertile, gives birth to sin." Their moral fall thus originated not in their creation but in their choice. Perfect beings could sin because freedom includes the potential for misuse.

Human Responsibility and Freedom

Jehovah's gift of free will is central to human dignity and moral accountability. Unlike the animals, who act according to instinct, humans are endowed with the capacity to reason, to discern right from wrong, and to make moral decisions (Proverbs 30:24; Joshua 24:15). This freedom defines the essence of what it means to be made in the image of God (Genesis 1:27).

However, freedom does not mean autonomy from moral law. True freedom exists only within the framework of truth and righteousness. Jesus said, "You will know the truth, and the truth will set you free" (John 8:32). To reject Jehovah's authority is not to attain liberty but to become enslaved to sin (Romans 6:16).

Jehovah desires voluntary love, not forced compliance. He is pleased when His creatures choose to love Him from the heart (Matthew 22:37–38). Satan, Adam, and Eve chose rebellion; each human must now choose whether to follow their path or return to Jehovah through Christ. The existence of moral evil is thus the inevitable consequence of free moral agency. The blame lies not with the Creator but with those who misuse His gift.

Does God Cause Us to Suffer?

Many who suffer ask, "Why has God done this to me?" Scripture provides a clear answer: "For a certainty, God does not act wickedly" (Job 34:12). James 1:13 elaborates: "When under trial, let no one say: 'I am being tried by God,' for with evil things God cannot be tried, nor does he himself try anyone." Jehovah neither causes evil nor tempts people to do wrong.

Suffering originates from three primary sources: human imperfection, chance, and the influence of Satan. Ecclesiastes 8:9 observes that humans often harm one another through selfishness and oppression. Ecclesiastes 9:11 adds that "time and unforeseen occurrence befall them all," meaning that calamity can strike anyone without moral cause. Above all, Scripture identifies Satan as "the ruler of this world" and "the god of this age" (John 12:31; 2 Corinthians 4:4). He is "the wicked one" who brings harm upon humanity (1 John 5:19). It is he, not Jehovah, who promotes disease, violence, immorality, and falsehood.

Jehovah permits suffering temporarily but never causes it. His allowance serves to fulfill the purpose of vindicating His sovereignty and exposing sin's destructive nature. Like a skilled physician allowing a painful treatment for healing's sake, God permits trials to bring about long-term good. The Christian, therefore, endures suffering not as punishment but as part of a fallen world under temporary rebellion.

The Temporal Versus Eternal Perspective

One of Scripture's great lessons is that human suffering must be viewed from the eternal perspective of God's purpose. Temporal pain cannot be compared with eternal glory. Paul, who endured imprisonment, beatings, and persecution, wrote, "For I consider that the sufferings of this present time are not worthy to be compared with the glory that is to be revealed in us" (Romans 8:18).

Jehovah's purpose is not to shield believers from every hardship but to shape them into Christlike maturity. Trials develop endurance, character, and hope (Romans 5:3–5). Through suffering, believers learn humility, compassion, and dependence upon God. From the eternal perspective, Jehovah's plan is not about temporary comfort but eternal restoration. The refining process of faith proves the genuineness of love for God, as gold is purified through fire (1 Peter 1:6–7).

Therefore, when Paul writes that "all things work together for good," he speaks of spiritual and eternal good—the good of conformity to Christ and participation in God's ultimate plan of redemption (Romans 8:29). Temporal suffering, when endured in faith, becomes the instrument by which eternal glory is achieved.

What Did Jesus Say About Suffering?

Jesus' ministry provides the clearest revelation of Jehovah's view of suffering. He did not attribute sickness, disaster, or poverty to divine punishment. Instead, He alleviated suffering through compassion and healing. "He healed the lame, the blind, the lepers, and the deaf" (Matthew 15:30). His miracles were not random acts of power but demonstrations of God's intent to remove suffering permanently.

When His disciples asked why a man was born blind, Jesus replied, "It was not that this man sinned, or his parents, but that the works of God might be displayed in him" (John 9:3). This statement overturns the false assumption that all suffering is divine retribution.

Jesus revealed that suffering can serve as a stage for God's glory and compassion.

Furthermore, Jesus identified Satan as "a manslayer when he began" (John 8:44) and as "the ruler of this world" (John 12:31). He exposed the true cause of suffering—the devil's rebellion and deceit. Yet He also announced the ultimate end of suffering through the coming Kingdom of God. In teaching His disciples to pray, "Let your Kingdom come," Jesus directed hope toward a future when God's will would be done "on earth as it is in heaven" (Matthew 6:10).

Jesus' death and resurrection guarantee this hope. Through His victory, He secured the promise of a restored creation where "death will be no more, neither will mourning nor outcry nor pain be anymore" (Revelation 21:4).

The Promise of Final Restoration

Jehovah's plan concludes not in defeat but in renewal. The present world, dominated by sin and suffering, will pass away, replaced by the new heavens and new earth foretold in Scripture (Isaiah 65:17; 2 Peter 3:13). Christ will reign until all enemies—including death—are destroyed (1 Corinthians 15:25–26).

For believers, this assurance transforms suffering into anticipation. Pain is temporary; restoration is eternal. Jehovah will vindicate His name, restore creation to perfection, and wipe every tear from His faithful ones' eyes.

Thus, the problem of evil finds its resolution not in philosophical abstraction but in the person of Jesus Christ and the fulfillment of God's purpose. Evil exists because of rebellion, continues by divine permission, and will end through divine restoration. Until that time, Jehovah causes all things—including suffering—to work together for eternal good for those who love Him.

Chapter 6 – The Witness of Creation

Main Verse: Psalm 19:1 – "The heavens are telling the glory of God; and the expanse is declaring the work of His hands."

General Revelation and Its Role in Convincing Reason

From the opening declaration of Psalm 19:1, the inspired psalmist proclaims the self-evident truth that the heavens continually declare the glory of God. Creation itself is not a mute monument to divine power but an ever-speaking testimony that appeals to human reason and conscience. This is what theologians call "general revelation"—the knowledge of God available to every person through what has been made. It is distinct from "special revelation," which comes through Scripture, yet it serves as a universal witness, leaving humanity without excuse. The apostle Paul confirms this in Romans 1:19–20, stating that what may be known about God is evident to all, for God made it evident through His works, so that people are without excuse.

General revelation functions as God's constant communication with His creatures. It is not limited by language, geography, or culture. The sun that rises on the righteous and the unrighteous alike (Matthew 5:45) and the intricate balance of ecosystems across the planet both proclaim the wisdom and goodness of the Creator. Even apart from Scripture, rational observation leads an honest mind to acknowledge a transcendent cause behind the order, beauty, and moral awareness inherent in the world. Such revelation does not save a person, but it serves to awaken in every conscience a recognition that God exists and that humanity is accountable to Him.

The Complexity and Order of the Universe

The universe displays a level of complexity and precision that no random process could reasonably account for. Every scientific discipline—from astronomy to molecular biology—testifies to an astonishing degree of order and interdependence. The fine-tuning of the cosmos, from the gravitational constant to the delicate balance of chemical and biological systems, reveals purpose and intelligence. The laws of physics and mathematics are not chaotic but consistent, intelligible, and universal. They point to a Lawgiver, not to chance.

When the Psalmist says that "the expanse is declaring the work of His hands," he captures the essence of this argument. The "expanse" refers to the heavens, the visible sky, and the cosmos beyond. The universe bears the fingerprints of design, coherence, and intention. The vast galaxies, though immeasurably distant, move in predictable courses, governed by constants that sustain the possibility of life on Earth. This harmony testifies that creation is not the product of impersonal forces but the expression of a personal, rational Creator—Jehovah, Who spoke the universe into being and sustains it by His power.

Modern discoveries in cosmology, far from undermining belief in God, have strengthened it. The more humanity learns about the intricacies of DNA, the precision of atomic structures, and the delicate balance of ecosystems, the clearer it becomes that creation is neither accidental nor autonomous. Science, properly understood, magnifies the glory of God by uncovering the wonders of His handiwork. Every equation solved and every mystery unveiled points back to the One Who ordered all things with purpose and intelligence.

The Design Argument in Biblical Perspective

The design argument, also known as the teleological argument, is not a modern invention but a deeply biblical concept. Scripture repeatedly calls upon creation as evidence of divine wisdom and power. In Isaiah 40:26, Jehovah challenges humanity to "lift up your eyes on high and see Who has created these stars, the One Who leads forth their host by number." The argument is simple yet profound: where there is design, there must be a Designer. This principle aligns with both reason and revelation.

Paul uses this very reasoning in Acts 14:17 when he tells the people of Lystra that God "did not leave Himself without witness, in that He did good and gave you rains from heaven and fruitful seasons." Creation, with its predictable cycles and life-sustaining order, is God's witness to all peoples. While fallen humanity often suppresses this truth in unrighteousness, it remains evident. The natural world, in all its splendor and complexity, reveals not only

God's existence but also His attributes—His eternal power, divine nature, wisdom, and goodness.

Biblically, this understanding of design is not an appeal to gaps in human knowledge but an acknowledgment of divine intentionality permeating every aspect of creation. The world is not self-created or self-sustaining; it depends continuously upon the will and power of its Maker. Colossians 1:16–17 teaches that all things were created through Christ and for Him, and that by Him all things hold together. The design argument, therefore, is not merely philosophical but deeply Christological. The same Word Who spoke all things into existence is the One Who maintains their order and purpose.

Creation's Testimony Against Atheistic Naturalism

Creation stands as a perpetual rebuke to atheistic naturalism, which asserts that the universe and life arose from impersonal matter and random processes. The biblical worldview, however, affirms that everything owes its origin to the personal Creator, Jehovah. The very concept of "natural law" presupposes order, predictability, and rationality—all of which demand an ultimate Lawgiver. Naturalism cannot account for these realities without borrowing from the theistic framework it rejects.

Atheistic naturalism fails because it denies the very foundation of reason. If human thought is merely the product of chemical reactions in the brain, then there is no basis for trusting reason, logic, or moral judgment. Yet every act of scientific inquiry assumes rational consistency and moral integrity—the expectation that truth exists and that it can be known. Such presuppositions make sense only in a universe created by a rational and moral Being.

Romans 1:21–23 reveals the moral root of naturalistic denial. It is not intellectual ignorance but willful suppression of truth that leads people to reject the Creator. Though they knew God through His works, they refused to glorify Him as God. Instead, they exchanged the truth of God for a lie and worshiped created things rather than the Creator. Creation testifies not only to God's existence but also to humanity's rebellion. The very existence of an orderly and beautiful world confronts every person with the reality of divine authorship, leaving no room for excuse.

Human Uniqueness and Moral Awareness

Among all created beings, humanity alone bears the image of God (Genesis 1:26–27). This means that human life possesses inherent dignity, rational capacity, and moral responsibility. While animals act by instinct, humans reason, create, and choose between right and wrong. Conscience itself is an aspect of general revelation—a divine implant that bears witness to moral accountability. Romans 2:14–15 affirms that even those who do not have the written Law of God show its work written on their hearts, their conscience bearing witness.

Human creativity, language, and moral reflection reveal an awareness of transcendence. People across all cultures demonstrate an innate sense of right and wrong, justice and injustice, good and evil. This moral awareness is not the result of evolutionary adaptation but of divine image-bearing. Every human being, even in a fallen state, retains a measure of moral awareness that reflects God's character, though distorted by sin.

The uniqueness of humanity also underscores the purpose of creation itself. The universe, vast and majestic, is the setting for human stewardship and worship. Jehovah made the world not for aimless existence but for His glory, that intelligent beings might know Him, honor Him, and reflect His righteousness. The rational and moral capacities of humans are designed for relationship with their Creator. This relationship, severed by sin, is restored only through Christ, the perfect image of God.

Creation as a Call to Worship

Creation not only reveals God's power and wisdom but also calls humanity to worship Him. The natural world inspires awe and reverence, directing the heart to its Maker. Psalm 8:3–4 captures this perfectly: "When I consider Your heavens, the work of Your fingers, the moon and the stars, which You have ordained; what is man that You take thought of him?" True worship arises when the created mind recognizes the majesty of the Creator and humbly submits to His authority.

The beauty of the heavens and the order of the earth were never meant to be ends in themselves. They point beyond themselves to the One Who fashioned them. Romans 11:36 declares, "For from Him and through Him and to Him are all things. To Him be the glory forever." Worship grounded in creation is not pantheistic admiration of nature but reverent acknowledgment of the Creator's glory manifested in what He has made.

Every sunrise is a sermon, every star a proclamation, every living thing a testimony that Jehovah reigns. Creation's witness is continuous, impartial, and universal. While fallen humanity distorts or ignores it, the faithful see in it a reason for gratitude and devotion. The wise man does not worship creation but worships the One Who made it. Thus, creation's ultimate purpose is doxological—it exists to bring glory to God and to invite His creatures to join in that praise.

In the end, the witness of creation confronts every human being with a decision: to glorify the Creator or to suppress His truth. Those who respond in humility and faith will find in special revelation—the Word of God—the fullness of that truth revealed in Jesus Christ. The heavens tell His glory, and His Word makes that glory known in saving power.

Chapter 7 – The Reliability of the Gospels

Main Verse: Luke 1:3–4 – "It seemed fitting for me... to write it out for you in consecutive order... so that you may know the exact truth."

The four Gospels—Matthew, Mark, Luke, and John—stand as the primary historical witnesses to the life, teachings, death, and resurrection of Jesus Christ. They are not theological fiction or allegory but carefully composed historical accounts grounded in eyewitness testimony and preserved through divine oversight. Luke's prologue affirms the historical intent behind the Gospels: "It seemed fitting for me... to write it out for you in consecutive order... so that you may know the exact truth" (Luke 1:3–4). The phrase "exact truth" (Greek: *asphaleian*) means certainty, reliability, or assurance.

Luke's purpose was not merely inspirational but evidential—he wrote to confirm the historical accuracy of the Christian message.

The reliability of the Gospels can be demonstrated through six essential areas: their eyewitness foundation, their harmony and individuality, archaeological and historical corroboration, textual preservation, the historical authenticity of Jesus' words and works, and the rational basis for faith rooted in evidence.

Eyewitness Testimony and Oral Tradition

The Gospels were written either by eyewitnesses of Jesus' ministry or by those who recorded eyewitness accounts under inspiration. Matthew and John were apostles who personally accompanied Jesus throughout His ministry. Mark, a close associate of Peter, wrote his Gospel from Peter's firsthand recollections (1 Peter 5:13; Papias' testimony as recorded by Eusebius). Luke, though not an eyewitness himself, compiled his account from those "who from the beginning were eyewitnesses and servants of the word" (Luke 1:2).

In the ancient world, oral transmission of information was highly disciplined. The Jewish culture of the first century relied heavily on memorization and public recitation, ensuring accurate preservation of teachings. The disciples, trained by Jesus Himself, transmitted His words with precision. Rabbis often taught through repetition and structured sayings, and Jesus employed similar methods—parables, parallelism, and poetic rhythm—to aid memory.

Furthermore, the Gospels were written while eyewitnesses were still alive, allowing for correction of any false claims. Paul's letters—some of which predate the written Gospels—affirm that hundreds of eyewitnesses to the resurrection were still living (1 Corinthians 15:6).

Thus, Christianity's historical claims were verifiable to its first readers. The apostolic testimony was not anonymous rumor but personal witness confirmed by those who knew the facts firsthand.

The Harmony and Distinctiveness of the Gospels

Critics sometimes claim that differences among the Gospels undermine their reliability. In reality, these variations demonstrate authenticity rather than contradiction. Each Gospel writer wrote from a distinct perspective and for a specific audience, emphasizing different aspects of Jesus' ministry under the guidance of the Holy Spirit.

Matthew, writing primarily to a Jewish audience, presents Jesus as the promised Messiah, the fulfillment of prophecy. Mark, addressing Roman readers, focuses on Jesus' actions and authority, portraying Him as the Servant-King who came to give His life as a ransom for many. Luke, the historian and physician, writes for Gentile readers, emphasizing Jesus' compassion, humanity, and the universality of salvation. John, writing later, provides a theological portrait that complements the synoptics, highlighting Jesus' divinity and eternal purpose.

Their collective witness forms a fourfold harmony that reflects the multifaceted reality of Jesus Christ. The differences in detail—such as order of events or emphasis—reflect perspective, not error. Just as four witnesses describing the same event from different vantage points provide a fuller understanding, so the Gospels together provide a complete and credible picture of the life of Christ. The unity of their core message and the integrity of their distinctions reveal a truthful historical record guided by divine inspiration.

Archaeological and Historical Confirmation

Archaeology and historical study have repeatedly confirmed the accuracy of the Gospel accounts. Far from being mythological or detached from reality, the Gospels reflect the precise political, cultural, and geographical context of first-century Palestine under Roman rule.

Luke, often regarded by historians as one of the most accurate ancient historians, identifies dozens of local officials, regions, and historical details that have been verified. For example, Luke refers to "Lysanias the tetrarch of Abilene" (Luke 3:1), a figure once doubted by scholars until inscriptions confirming his existence were discovered near Damascus. Likewise, Luke's mention of "politarchs" in Thessalonica (Acts 17:6) was confirmed through archaeological evidence, even though the title was unknown outside the Bible until the nineteenth century.

Excavations in Jerusalem, Capernaum, and Nazareth have verified the existence of locations and customs described in the Gospels. The Pool of Bethesda, where Jesus healed the lame man (John 5:2), was once considered mythical until archaeologists uncovered its five porticoes exactly as John described. The ossuary of Caiaphas, the high priest who condemned Jesus, was discovered in 1990, providing direct historical connection to the Gospel narrative.

Furthermore, Roman records confirm the governance of Pontius Pilate, the use of crucifixion as a form of execution, and the social structures described throughout the New Testament. These confirmations demonstrate that the Gospel writers were reporting verifiable history, not constructing theological legends.

Transmission and Preservation of the Text

The textual transmission of the Gospels is unparalleled in ancient literature. The New Testament is supported by over 5,898 Greek manuscripts, in addition to 10,000 Latin manuscripts and more than 9,000 in other early languages. By comparison, most classical works survive in only a handful of manuscripts—often separated by centuries from the originals.

The earliest fragments of the Gospels date within decades of their composition. The Rylands Papyrus (P52), containing a portion of John 18:31–33, 37–38, is dated around 125 C.E., demonstrating that John's Gospel circulated widely within a generation of the apostle's lifetime. The Chester Beatty and Bodmer papyri, dated to the second and third centuries, preserve substantial portions of all four Gospels.

Through careful comparison of thousands of manuscripts, textual scholars have restored the New Testament text to more than 99.9% accuracy relative to the autographs. Variations that exist are minor—spelling differences, word order, or scribal slips—and do not affect doctrine or meaning. While Jehovah did not preserve the physical manuscripts, He ensured through providence that the content of His inspired Word was faithfully transmitted and restored. The reliability of the Gospels, therefore, is not merely theological but textual.

Jesus' Words and Works as Historical Realities

The Gospels record not mythic embellishments but genuine historical events. Jesus' teachings, miracles, and resurrection appearances are attested by multiple sources, including hostile or neutral witnesses. Even opponents acknowledged His works—some attributing them to demonic power (Matthew 12:24)—thereby confirming their reality.

Jesus' moral teaching bears all the marks of authenticity. His parables, ethical commands, and divine claims reflect an originality and authority unparalleled in human history. His moral perfection, recorded by those closest to Him, aligns with His divine identity. Unlike mythological heroes, Jesus' portrayal is consistent, sober, and free of exaggeration.

The central claim of the Gospels—the resurrection—is the linchpin of their reliability. The tomb was empty; the disciples were transformed; and the early church's existence demands explanation. No natural theory adequately accounts for these facts. The Gospels, written within the lifetime of eyewitnesses, record these events not as metaphor but as verifiable history. As Luke states, Jesus "presented Himself alive after His suffering, by many convincing proofs" (Acts 1:3).

Faith Founded on Evidence

Christian faith is not credulity but conviction based on evidence. Luke's purpose was to provide Theophilus—and every believer thereafter—certainty about the truth of the Gospel message. The Greek term *asphaleia* denotes stability and assurance, emphasizing that faith rests upon a solid foundation of fact. Jehovah never calls for blind belief but for informed trust grounded in His revealed Word.

The apostolic faith was consistently evidential. Peter urged believers to be ready "to make a defense to everyone who asks you to give an account for the hope that is in you" (1 Peter 3:15). The early Christians proclaimed a risen Savior, not as myth but as history. The harmony of the Gospels, the corroboration of archaeology, the preservation of the text, and the internal moral and theological coherence of their message all testify to divine truth.

The Gospels stand as Jehovah's inspired record of His Son's redemptive work. They reveal Jesus Christ not as an abstract figure of devotion but as the incarnate Word who entered history, died for sin, and rose from the dead. Their reliability ensures that faith in Him is not misplaced sentiment but a response to historical and spiritual reality. To trust the Gospels is to stand upon the sure foundation of truth revealed, verified, and preserved by God Himself.

Chapter 8 – The Reality of the Resurrection

Main Verse: 1 Corinthians 15:14 – "And if Christ has not been raised, then our preaching is vain, your faith also is vain."

The resurrection of Jesus Christ stands as the central event of Christian faith—the cornerstone upon which all doctrine, hope, and salvation rest. Without it, Christianity collapses into mere philosophy or moralism, devoid of redemptive power. Paul's words in 1 Corinthians 15:14 strike at the core of this reality: "And if Christ has not been raised, then our preaching is vain, your faith also is vain." The resurrection is not a symbolic tale or mystical metaphor; it is an historical event that validates every claim of Jesus and confirms the truth of the Gospel.

From the beginning, the apostles preached a risen Christ as the decisive proof of His divinity and the certainty of human resurrection. The Christian proclamation did not begin with abstract theology but with the eyewitness declaration: "He is risen!" The resurrection affirms that Jehovah's power conquered death, vindicated His Son, and guaranteed eternal life to all who believe. The evidence for the resurrection is abundant, rational, and consistent—rooted in historical fact, confirmed by eyewitnesses, and transformative in its effects.

The Empty Tomb: Historical and Logical Necessity

The first and most fundamental fact of the resurrection is the empty tomb. All four Gospels report that on the third day after Jesus' execution, His tomb was found empty by the women who had come to anoint His body (Matthew 28:1–7; Mark 16:1–6; Luke 24:1–3; John 20:1–8). This event is foundational, for if the tomb were not empty, the claim of resurrection could have been immediately refuted by the authorities.

The burial and sealing of the tomb are themselves historically verified. Jesus' body was placed in the new tomb of Joseph of Arimathea, a member of the Sanhedrin, ensuring that its location was publicly known (Matthew 27:57–61). The Romans sealed the tomb and stationed guards there (Matthew 27:62–66), making human tampering highly improbable. Yet by Sunday morning, the stone was rolled away, the body was gone, and the grave clothes were left behind, folded neatly (John 20:6–7).

No credible explanation has ever been given for the empty tomb apart from the resurrection. The Jewish leaders admitted its emptiness but claimed that the disciples had stolen the body (Matthew 28:11–15). However, such an explanation collapses under scrutiny. The disciples were terrified, in hiding, and completely demoralized. It is psychologically implausible that they would risk death to perpetuate a lie. Moreover, grave robbery could not account for the orderly state of the burial linens or the transformation of the disciples from fear to boldness.

The empty tomb stands as historical and logical necessity. Both friend and foe acknowledged it; the question is not whether the tomb was empty, but why. The resurrection provides the only explanation consistent with the evidence and with the subsequent rise of the Christian movement.

The Post-Resurrection Appearances

After His resurrection, Jesus appeared to numerous individuals and groups under varying circumstances, eliminating any theory of hallucination or myth. The Gospels and Epistles record multiple distinct appearances over a forty-day period before His ascension.

He appeared first to Mary Magdalene near the tomb (John 20:14–18), then to other women returning from the tomb (Matthew 28:9–10), to Peter (Luke 24:34), to two disciples on the road to Emmaus (Luke 24:13–32), to the gathered apostles without Thomas (John 20:19–23), and then with Thomas present (John 20:26–29). Paul adds further appearances to over five hundred brethren at one time, to James, and finally to himself (1 Corinthians 15:6–8).

These appearances were physical and verifiable, not mere visions or spiritual impressions. Jesus invited Thomas to touch His wounds (John 20:27) and ate with the disciples to prove His bodily presence (Luke 24:41–43). His resurrected body was glorified yet tangible, demonstrating that resurrection is not disembodied existence but restored and perfected life.

The diversity of these encounters—private and public, indoors and outdoors, to men and women, to believers and skeptics—rules out the possibility of collective delusion. The disciples were neither expecting nor predisposed to believe in His resurrection; their initial reaction was disbelief (Luke 24:11). Only the undeniable reality of encountering the risen Christ could have transformed their skepticism into unwavering conviction.

The Transformation of the Apostles

The transformation of the apostles is one of the most compelling evidences for the resurrection. Before Jesus' death, they were fearful and disheartened, fleeing at His arrest and hiding in despair. Yet within weeks, these same men stood before hostile authorities proclaiming boldly that Jesus had risen from the dead. Peter, who had denied Him three times, now declared to the crowds in Jerusalem, "This Jesus God raised up, and of that we all are witnesses" (Acts 2:32).

Such radical change demands an adequate cause. No psychological theory—such as wishful thinking or grief-induced hallucination—can explain the courage and consistency of the apostles' testimony. They proclaimed the resurrection in the very city where Jesus had been crucified, in the presence of those who could have disproven it. Moreover, they persisted in this proclamation despite persecution, imprisonment, and martyrdom.

Men may die for beliefs they hold sincerely but are mistaken about; they will not die for what they know to be a falsehood. The apostles' willingness to suffer and die for their testimony proves their absolute certainty that they had seen the risen Christ. Their courage was the fruit of conviction grounded in firsthand experience, not legend or imagination.

The Birth of the Early Church

The resurrection is not merely an isolated miracle; it is the catalyst for the birth of the Christian church. Within weeks of Jesus' crucifixion, thousands of Jews in Jerusalem—many of whom had witnessed His death—embraced faith in Him as the Messiah and were baptized (Acts 2:41). The explosive growth of the church, beginning in the very city where He was executed, is inexplicable apart from the resurrection.

The content of early Christian preaching was not ethical reform or abstract theology but the proclamation of a risen Savior. The apostles' message centered on one fact: "God raised Him from the dead" (Acts 3:15). The resurrection was the proof of divine validation—the evidence that Jesus' death was not defeat but victory over sin and death. Every sermon in the book of Acts revolves around this event. The early believers' worship on the first day of the week rather than the Sabbath also reflects the decisive impact of the resurrection on their faith and practice.

The existence of the church as a global and enduring movement testifies to the power of that historical event. No human scheme or myth could produce such lasting transformation across nations, languages, and centuries. The resurrection alone provides an adequate explanation for the church's origin and endurance.

Alternative Explanations Examined

Throughout history, skeptics have proposed alternative theories to explain the resurrection. Yet each fails under careful examination.

The Swoon Theory suggests that Jesus merely fainted and later revived. This is untenable. Roman executioners were experts in death, and the spear thrust into Jesus' side ensured His demise (John 19:34).

Moreover, a half-dead man could not have rolled away a massive stone or inspired His disciples to worship Him as the glorified Son of God.

The Theft Theory, promoted by the Jewish authorities, claims that the disciples stole the body (Matthew 28:13). Yet the disciples had neither motive, opportunity, nor courage to attempt such an act. Their despair and fear make the notion of a deliberate fraud impossible. Furthermore, the Roman guard and official seal rendered the tomb secure.

The Hallucination Theory fails to account for group appearances and physical interactions with Jesus. Hallucinations are subjective and individual; they cannot be experienced by groups under diverse circumstances.

The Myth Theory posits that the resurrection was a later legend. However, the early creeds of the New Testament (such as 1 Corinthians 15:3–8) show that belief in the resurrection was established within a few years of the event—far too early for mythic development. The writings of the apostles, composed within the first century, consistently present the resurrection as historical fact, not allegory.

No natural explanation satisfies the evidence. The resurrection remains the only conclusion that accounts for the empty tomb, the eyewitness testimony, the transformation of the apostles, and the birth of the early church.

The Resurrection as the Seal of Salvation

The resurrection is not only historical; it is theological and redemptive. It is the seal upon the completed work of Christ's atonement. His death paid the penalty for sin; His resurrection proved that the payment was accepted by Jehovah. Paul writes, "He was delivered over because of our transgressions and was raised because of our justification" (Romans 4:25). The resurrection is thus God's declaration that the sacrifice of His Son fully satisfied divine justice.

Moreover, the resurrection guarantees the believer's own future resurrection. Jesus proclaimed, "Because I live, you will live also" (John 14:19). His victory over death transformed the grave from a place of despair into the gateway of eternal life. The same power that raised Christ now works in those who believe, ensuring that death no longer has dominion over them (Romans 6:9).

The resurrection also establishes Jesus' authority as Lord. Having conquered death, He reigns as the living Christ who intercedes for His followers (Romans 8:34). Faith in a dead prophet cannot save; faith in a living Savior does.

For this reason, the resurrection remains the unshakable foundation of Christian faith. It is not a doctrine among others but the reality upon which all others depend. Through it, Jehovah vindicated His Son, confirmed His Word, and secured redemption for humanity.

The reality of the resurrection demands both belief and transformation. To know that Christ is risen is to recognize that His power continues to change lives today. The same Spirit who raised Him now calls every person to repentance and faith, promising eternal life to those who follow the risen Lord.

Chapter 9 – Faith and the Mind

Main Verse: Matthew 22:37 – "You shall love the Lord your God with all your heart, and with all your soul, and with all your mind."

The Biblical Call to Intellectual Engagement

Faith in God is not an escape from the use of the mind, nor does it require blind submission devoid of understanding. When Jesus declared that we are to love Jehovah with all our heart, soul, and mind, He affirmed that genuine devotion must encompass the full range of human faculties. The believer is called to engage intellectually, not to suppress thought. Scripture never separates faith from reason but commands the integration of both under the authority of divine revelation. True biblical faith involves trust grounded in truth. God expects His people to know what they believe and why they believe it.

From the earliest chapters of Scripture, Jehovah communicates with humanity through language, appealing to man's rational capacity. Adam was created with intellect and moral discernment. God reasoned with Cain about his anger (Genesis 4:6–7), and later He reasoned with Israel through the prophets, saying, "Come now, and let us reason together" (Isaiah 1:18). The very act of divine revelation presupposes that human beings can understand and respond rationally to God's words. Thus, loving God with one's mind means studying His Word diligently, examining His works attentively, and submitting one's reasoning to the illumination of His truth.

Reason as a Gift of God

Reason itself is not a product of human evolution or cultural advancement; it is a divine endowment. When Jehovah created man in His image (Genesis 1:26–27), He imparted intellect, moral awareness, and the ability to communicate logically. The mind is therefore a sacred trust, intended for discerning truth and making choices consistent with God's will. The misuse of reason does not discredit reason itself any more than the abuse of freedom invalidates liberty. The fall into sin corrupted human reasoning (Romans 1:21–22), but redemption through Christ restores the capacity to think rightly when the mind is renewed by God's Word.

Scripture teaches that believers are not to abandon logic but to purify it through submission to divine revelation. Proverbs 2:6 states, "For Jehovah gives wisdom; from His mouth come knowledge and understanding." Here wisdom, knowledge, and understanding are not worldly constructs but spiritual gifts originating from God's own nature. This means the Christian's intellect is to be governed by

Scripture, disciplined by humility, and directed toward the glory of God. The believer's reasoning becomes an act of worship when it is exercised within the bounds of divine truth.

The Harmony Between Faith and Logic

Faith and logic are not adversaries but companions when rightly ordered. Biblical faith is trust in the testimony of God, Who cannot lie (Titus 1:2). Logic, on the other hand, is the means by which we discern coherence and consistency. Since God is the Author of both Scripture and rational order, His revelation cannot contradict sound reasoning. The apostle Paul reasoned in the synagogues and marketplaces (Acts 17:2, 17), demonstrating that faith in Christ can be logically defended and intellectually satisfying.

The harmony between faith and logic is illustrated in creation itself. The universe operates according to rational, discoverable laws because it was designed by a rational Creator. Science, mathematics, and philosophy all presuppose an orderly and intelligible world. This intelligibility is not self-generated but flows from Jehovah's wisdom. Therefore, when Christians engage in scientific or philosophical inquiry, they are not stepping outside of faith but exploring the order that God has established.

Faith does not contradict reason; it transcends it by resting on the infallible Word of God rather than the shifting opinions of men. Hebrews 11:1 defines faith as "the assurance of things hoped for, the conviction of things not seen." This is not irrational credulity but confidence in the character and promises of God. The Christian's faith is reasonable because it is grounded in evidence—historical, moral, and experiential—that points to the truthfulness of Scripture.

Edward D. Andrews

The Dangers of Anti-Intellectual Christianity

A grave danger in modern Christianity is the rejection of intellectual rigor. Many professing believers have substituted emotionalism, tradition, or human authority for the disciplined study of Scripture. This anti-intellectual spirit weakens the church, leaving it vulnerable to false teaching and cultural compromise. Paul warned Timothy to "retain the standard of sound words" (2 Timothy 1:13) and to handle "the word of truth" accurately (2 Timothy 2:15). This requires study, discernment, and the application of logic guided by the Holy Spirit's inspired Word.

When believers neglect the intellectual dimension of faith, they lose the ability to distinguish truth from error. Emotional experience becomes the measure of authenticity rather than doctrinal soundness. This distortion breeds spiritual immaturity and opens the door to deception. The mind must not be abandoned in pursuit of spiritual fervor, for zeal without knowledge leads to ruin (Romans 10:2). A mature Christian faith integrates heart and intellect in obedience to God's revelation.

Jehovah calls His people to test all things and hold fast to what is good (1 Thessalonians 5:21). This testing involves rational evaluation based on Scripture. The church must therefore cultivate a culture of sound teaching, where the Word of God governs belief and practice. The anti-intellectual trend in modern religion undermines the authority of Scripture and replaces divine revelation with subjective opinion. Genuine spirituality is not found in rejecting the mind but in renewing it through truth.

Renewing the Mind Through Truth

The apostle Paul exhorts believers to "be transformed by the renewing of your mind" (Romans 12:2). This renewal is not mystical or automatic; it comes through deliberate exposure to God's Word and obedience to its principles. The fallen mind is darkened by sin and must be continually purified through the study and meditation of Scripture. The Word of God acts as both a mirror and a lamp—revealing the true condition of the heart and illuminating the path of righteousness.

Renewal of the mind begins with repentance, which involves a change in thinking that aligns one's will with God's. This process continues as believers internalize divine truth, allowing it to shape their worldview. Philippians 4:8 instructs Christians to dwell on whatever is true, honorable, right, pure, lovely, and commendable. This command directs thought toward that which reflects the character of God. A renewed mind produces discernment, enabling believers to recognize false philosophies, moral corruption, and spiritual deception.

The Scriptures repeatedly warn against the corruption of the mind by worldly influences. Colossians 2:8 cautions believers: "See to it that no one takes you captive through philosophy and empty deception, according to human tradition, according to the elementary principles of the world, rather than according to Christ." The antidote to this captivity is a mind anchored in the unchanging truth of God's Word. The renewed intellect submits to Christ's lordship, discerning all things through the lens of divine revelation.

Wisdom Versus Worldly Speculation

True wisdom is inseparable from the fear of Jehovah. Proverbs 9:10 declares, "The fear of Jehovah is the beginning of wisdom, and the knowledge of the Holy One is understanding." The world claims to offer wisdom through philosophy, science, and culture, yet its wisdom is grounded in human pride and rebellion against God. James contrasts this earthly wisdom with the wisdom from above, which is "first pure, then peaceable, gentle, reasonable, full of mercy and good fruits, unwavering, without hypocrisy" (James 3:17).

Worldly speculation exalts human opinion over divine truth. The philosophies of materialism, relativism, and naturalism all attempt to explain existence apart from God. These systems, though intellectually impressive, are spiritually bankrupt because they begin with a false premise: that man is autonomous and truth is self-defined. In contrast, biblical wisdom begins with submission to God's authority. It recognizes that all truth is God's truth and that reason finds its fulfillment only in Him.

The believer must therefore resist the temptation to conform his thinking to the world. Paul warned the Corinthians not to rely on the "wisdom of men" but on "the power of God" (1 Corinthians 2:5). He demonstrated that human philosophy, detached from revelation, cannot lead to salvation or moral transformation. The cross of Christ stands as the ultimate contradiction to worldly reasoning—foolishness to the unregenerate mind, yet the power and wisdom of God to those who believe (1 Corinthians 1:18–24).

To love God with the mind is to subject every thought to His authority (2 Corinthians 10:5). This involves intellectual humility, the recognition that human reason is finite and dependent on divine illumination. The Christian thinker must guard against pride, remembering that knowledge without love "puffs up" (1 Corinthians 8:1). True knowledge leads to worship, gratitude, and obedience. Faithful reasoning glorifies God because it acknowledges Him as the source of all wisdom and truth.

REASONABLE FAITH

The integration of faith and intellect is not optional but essential to spiritual maturity. Jehovah desires a people who think His thoughts after Him, who discern truth from error, and who reflect His wisdom in every area of life. The mind renewed by Scripture becomes a vessel through which God's truth is proclaimed and defended in a darkened world. To love God with the mind is to dedicate every intellectual pursuit to His glory, using reason as a servant of faith and truth as the foundation of understanding.

Chapter 10 – The Role of the Holy Spirit

Main Verse: John 16:13 – "When He, the Spirit of truth, comes, He will guide you into all the truth."

The Spirit's Work Through the Word

The Holy Spirit is the divine Agent of Truth Who operates exclusively through the written Word of God. Jesus Christ assured His disciples that "the Spirit of truth" would come to "guide you into all the truth" (John 16:13). This promise found its primary fulfillment in the apostles, who were directly inspired to record the New Testament Scriptures. Therefore, the Spirit's role in the life of the believer today is not to provide new revelation or personal mystical experiences but to bring understanding, conviction, and direction through the divinely inspired Scriptures. The Spirit inspired the biblical authors in such a way that "men spoke from God as they were carried along by the Holy Spirit" (2 Peter 1:21).

The Spirit's work through the Word demonstrates Jehovah's orderly and rational method of communication. From the beginning, Jehovah revealed His will through spoken and written revelation. The Holy Spirit's role in inspiration was unique and completed with the close of the apostolic era. What remains is the Spirit's continued illumination of the already revealed Word, enabling sincere readers to grasp the intended meaning of Scripture. The Holy Spirit does not implant ideas, whisper revelations, or bypass the human mind; rather, He guides understanding as the believer diligently studies, meditates upon, and applies Scripture.

It is crucial to distinguish between revelation, inspiration, and illumination. Revelation refers to God's disclosure of divine truth previously unknown to humanity. Inspiration refers to the Spirit's act of superintending the biblical writers so that their writings were the inerrant Word of God. Illumination refers to the Spirit's help in understanding the meaning of what has been revealed and inspired. The Spirit's present activity in believers centers entirely on illumination, never on revelation or inspiration, since those functions concluded when the canon of Scripture was completed near the end of the first century C.E.

The Spirit's Conviction of Sin and Assurance of Truth

One of the most vital aspects of the Spirit's work through the Word is His conviction of sin. Jesus said, "When He comes, He will convict the world concerning sin and righteousness and judgment" (John 16:8). The Spirit accomplishes this not through mystical feelings or supernatural visions but through the power of Scripture. Hebrews 4:12 states that "the word of God is living and active, sharper than any two-edged sword." This living Word, breathed out by the Spirit, exposes the inner condition of the heart, revealing humanity's sinfulness and need for salvation through Christ.

Conviction is not the same as condemnation. The Spirit convicts to bring repentance, not despair. Condemnation belongs to those who reject the truth (John 3:18), while conviction is the gracious act of God that opens the eyes of sinners to see their spiritual need. Through the Spirit's convicting power, individuals are drawn to the truth of the gospel and persuaded of its veracity. The Spirit thus operates as the divine Prosecutor, confronting the unbeliever with the reality of sin and the righteousness of Christ.

For believers, the Spirit provides assurance of truth through Scripture. When a person accepts the authority of God's Word and responds in faith to its message, the Spirit confirms that understanding within the mind and conscience, bringing peace that stems from alignment with divine truth. The Spirit assures believers that the Scriptures they study are not the words of men but of God. This assurance is intellectual, moral, and spiritual, not emotional or mystical. The believer knows that what is written in Scripture is true because the Spirit, Who authored the Word, testifies to its truthfulness within the renewed mind.

The Spirit's Testimony to Jesus Christ

The Holy Spirit's primary purpose is to bear witness to Jesus Christ, not to Himself. In John 15:26, Jesus declared, "When the Helper comes, whom I will send to you from the Father, the Spirit of truth who proceeds from the Father, He will bear witness about Me." This is the central focus of the Spirit's ministry. He glorifies Christ by directing believers' attention to the Person, work, and teachings of Jesus as revealed in Scripture.

This testimony is objective and centered on the Word. The Spirit magnifies the Son by enabling believers to understand the Scriptures that testify about Him. From Genesis to Revelation, the Word of God reveals the redemptive plan culminating in Jesus Christ. The Spirit's testimony is not experienced through subjective impulses but through the comprehension of inspired truth. When believers read Scripture and perceive its Christ-centered unity, they are witnessing the Spirit's testimony at work.

The Spirit also bears witness to the authenticity and sufficiency of Christ's atonement. Romans 8:16 states, "The Spirit Himself bears witness with our spirit that we are children of God." This witness is not a mystical whisper but the rational confirmation that arises from Scripture's truthfulness. The Spirit testifies through the written record that Christ's sacrifice is sufficient, His resurrection is factual, and His promises are sure. The Spirit glorifies Christ by exalting His Word and affirming that redemption has been fully accomplished through Him alone.

Illumination, Not Inspiration for Believers

Many confuse the Spirit's illumination with inspiration, but Scripture carefully differentiates the two. Inspiration refers to the Spirit's action in producing the Bible, whereas illumination refers to His work in helping believers understand it. No Christian today is inspired in the biblical sense, for inspiration resulted in the infallible recording of God's revelation—a process completed in the first century. Illumination, on the other hand, continues as the Spirit enables comprehension of divine truth.

Illumination occurs when the believer studies the Word with a submissive heart and an obedient will. The Spirit does not impose understanding apart from diligent study; He enlightens the mind as one reads, meditates, and compares Scripture with Scripture. The Spirit's illumination ensures that the text speaks as intended by its divine Author, not according to human imagination. The Holy Spirit thus guards the believer from misinterpretation and error by drawing the mind back to the plain, literal meaning of Scripture as understood in its grammatical and historical context.

It must be emphasized that illumination does not equate to revelation. The Spirit does not reveal new doctrines or disclose personal guidance outside of Scripture. Rather, He enables believers to grasp, apply, and obey the truths already revealed. When a Christian grows in understanding, it is not because new light has been revealed but because the Spirit has enabled deeper comprehension of the existing light of God's Word.

The Spirit's illumination also requires moral and spiritual submission. A disobedient or prideful heart will not perceive truth clearly, for the Spirit grants insight to those who are humble, reverent, and obedient to God's will. Psalm 25:9 declares, "He leads the humble in what is right and teaches the humble His way." The Spirit's illumination is not mechanical; it is relational, depending upon the believer's willingness to obey the Word being studied. Thus, illumination is both intellectual and moral—an act of divine grace that rewards sincere study and submission to Scripture.

The Spirit's Role in Defending Faith

The Holy Spirit equips believers to defend the Christian faith through the accurate understanding and application of Scripture. In a world hostile to biblical truth, the Spirit strengthens believers to stand firm upon the foundation of the Word. Jesus promised that the Spirit would empower His followers to bear witness to the truth (Acts 1:8). However, this empowerment operates through the believer's knowledge of Scripture, not through ecstatic experiences or emotional impulses.

The Spirit is the divine Author of Scripture, and therefore the defender of truth must rely upon the Spirit's Word as the final authority. When believers use Scripture in defense of the faith, they are aligning with the Spirit's own method of testifying to the truth. The Spirit never contradicts the Word He inspired; He never leads one to compromise biblical authority for the sake of cultural acceptance. Through Scripture, the Spirit provides the foundation for sound doctrine, moral conviction, and evangelistic confidence.

Apologetics grounded in the Spirit's Word differs sharply from human philosophy. Human reasoning apart from Scripture leads to confusion, but reasoning shaped by divine revelation produces conviction and clarity. The Spirit does not argue apart from the Word; He argues through it. When a believer quotes, explains, and applies the Bible in defense of truth, the Spirit's sword is wielded effectively. As Paul wrote, "The sword of the Spirit... is the word of God" (Ephesians 6:17).

The Spirit's role in defending faith also involves equipping the church collectively. When believers assemble around the teaching of Scripture, the Spirit unites them in truth and fortifies them against error. Through the faithful exposition of Scripture, the Spirit strengthens the minds and hearts of the congregation, enabling them to discern false doctrine and to respond to opposition with gentleness and respect (1 Peter 3:15). In this way, the Spirit sustains the church's witness in a hostile world and ensures that the truth of the gospel continues uncorrupted from generation to generation.

Living by the Guidance of the Scriptures

To live by the guidance of the Spirit is to live by the guidance of the Scriptures, for the Spirit and the Word are inseparably united. The Spirit inspired the Word, illuminates the mind to understand it, and empowers obedience to it. Therefore, the believer who desires to walk by the Spirit must walk according to the revealed Word of God. Paul wrote, "If we live by the Spirit, let us also keep in step with the Spirit" (Galatians 5:25). To keep in step with the Spirit means to align one's life with the moral and doctrinal teachings of Scripture.

The Spirit's guidance is not an inward feeling but a Scriptural direction. Jehovah has provided in His Word every principle necessary for righteous living. The Spirit brings these principles to remembrance as believers apply them to daily circumstances. For instance, when facing temptation, the Spirit recalls Scripture to mind, just as He did for Jesus during His temptation in the wilderness (Matthew 4:1–11). The Spirit does not override the believer's mind but renews it through truth so that decisions are made according to God's revealed will.

Living by the Spirit's guidance also entails dependence upon His strength to obey the Word. The Spirit empowers believers to resist sin, to love righteousness, and to serve faithfully. This empowerment is not mystical possession but moral transformation produced by the truth. Jesus prayed, "Sanctify them in the truth; Your word is truth" (John 17:17). The Spirit accomplishes sanctification by applying that Word to the believer's life, convicting of wrongdoing, and prompting repentance and obedience.

Thus, the Spirit's role in the believer's life is not to provide emotional experiences or supernatural revelations but to make the Word effective. Through the Spirit's illumination, conviction, and empowerment, the believer is transformed into Christ's likeness.

True spirituality, therefore, is measured not by ecstatic experiences but by conformity to the written Word of God. The Spirit-filled life is a Scripture-filled life.

In every generation, believers must resist the tendency to separate the Spirit from the Word. Many claim spiritual guidance while disregarding the authority of Scripture, but this divorces the Spirit from the very instrument He uses. The Spirit never guides contrary to the Bible; He always guides through it. To be Spirit-led is to be Word-governed. The Holy Spirit's work is to glorify Christ by exalting His Word, convicting the world of sin, illuminating the truth, and empowering obedience. Therefore, those who seek to live by the Spirit must anchor their lives entirely upon the Scriptures He inspired.

Chapter 11 – Overcoming Intellectual Barriers

Main Verse: 2 Corinthians 10:5 – "We are destroying speculations and every lofty thing raised up against the knowledge of God."

The Apostle Paul's declaration in 2 Corinthians 10:5 establishes the spiritual and intellectual foundation for Christian apologetics. It is not a defensive retreat but a confident demolition of falsehoods opposed to the knowledge of God. Christianity is not anti-intellectual; rather, it demands that every thought be made captive to the obedience of Christ. The Christian faith, when rightly understood, is intellectually superior, morally pure, and spiritually liberating. The gospel of Christ provides the only coherent worldview that unites truth, meaning, and moral grounding.

Common Philosophical Objections to Christianity

Many intellectual barriers arise not from evidence against Christianity but from misconceptions about what Christianity teaches and from the human inclination toward autonomy from God. Among the most prominent objections are the claims that reason and science have made faith obsolete, that evil disproves God's goodness, that religion is merely cultural or psychological, and that all truth is relative. Each of these challenges, when examined through sound reasoning and Scripture, collapses under the weight of its own inconsistency.

Secular humanism assumes that man is capable of determining truth and morality apart from divine revelation. However, without God, there can be no objective foundation for moral or rational judgments. If the universe is merely a product of random material forces, then human reasoning itself is nothing more than the by-product of chemical reactions, and truth cannot exist. The consistent Christian apologist must expose these contradictions and demonstrate that all human knowledge presupposes the existence of a rational Creator.

The Christian worldview affirms that reason and revelation are not enemies but allies. Since man is made in the image of God, endowed with rationality, his intellectual capacities reflect God's own orderly mind. The unbeliever's problem is not lack of evidence but suppression of truth (Romans 1:18–20). The Christian's task is to remove intellectual barriers that obscure the clear testimony of God's Word and creation, showing that unbelief is irrational at its core.

The Limits of Human Understanding

A fundamental problem in philosophy is epistemology—the study of how we know what we know. Human reason, while valuable, is finite and fallen. Sin has corrupted not only man's heart but also his intellect (Ephesians 4:17–18). Thus, unaided human reason cannot fully apprehend divine truth. The intellect is a marvelous instrument, but when separated from divine revelation, it leads to futility.

Philosophers throughout history have wrestled with the limitations of human understanding. From Socrates' acknowledgment of ignorance to Kant's skepticism about metaphysical knowledge, mankind's inability to reach certainty apart from revelation has been evident. Christianity, however, provides the answer: true knowledge begins with the fear of Jehovah (Proverbs 1:7). The believer recognizes that all truth is grounded in the character and revelation of God.

This does not mean that faith replaces reason, but that faith perfects reason by providing its necessary foundation. Reason without revelation is like a lamp without oil—capable of shining only momentarily before it is extinguished. The humility to acknowledge human limitation opens the way to divine illumination. As Paul wrote, "The world through its wisdom did not come to know God" (1 Corinthians 1:21). Human intellect, when autonomous, leads to pride and confusion; but when submitted to Christ, it becomes a powerful instrument for proclaiming truth.

Refuting Naturalism and Materialism

Naturalism and materialism form the philosophical backbone of atheism. They assert that reality consists solely of physical matter and that all phenomena—including thought, morality, and consciousness—can be explained by natural processes. However, these worldviews collapse under logical scrutiny.

If materialism is true, then human thoughts are merely chemical reactions determined by physical laws. In that case, no thought, including belief in materialism itself, could be rationally justified. Rational inference requires freedom of the mind from physical determinism. The ability to reason presupposes an immaterial aspect of man—a soul created by God. Moreover, moral values, abstract logic, and mathematical truths cannot be reduced to physical properties. They are non-material realities that point directly to a transcendent, immaterial Creator.

The Christian worldview affirms both the physical and the spiritual. God created the material universe, but He Himself is not bound by it. Matter has meaning because it is the handiwork of an intelligent Designer. The order and intelligibility of the cosmos bear witness to Jehovah's rational nature (Psalm 19:1). Science itself depends on the assumption that the universe operates according to stable laws—an assumption that only makes sense in a theistic framework.

The rise of modern science in the sixteenth and seventeenth centuries was not born from atheism but from biblical conviction. Men like Kepler, Newton, and Pascal believed that the universe was created by a rational God whose works could be studied and understood. Naturalism, by contrast, destroys the very foundation upon which scientific inquiry rests. Without God, there can be no assurance that the human mind is capable of discerning truth or that the universe follows consistent patterns.

Edward D. Andrews

The Moral Argument for God's Existence

One of the most compelling evidences for God is the existence of objective moral values and duties. Every human being recognizes a distinction between right and wrong. Even those who deny moral absolutes live as if certain actions—such as murder or betrayal—are universally wrong. This moral awareness cannot be explained by evolutionary or cultural conditioning, for such theories fail to account for the *oughtness* of moral obligation.

If morality were merely a product of human evolution, it would have no binding authority. What is morally right would simply be what promotes survival, and cruelty could be justified if it served evolutionary advantage. But man's conscience testifies to a higher law written on the heart (Romans 2:14–15). This moral lawgiver is Jehovah, whose righteousness is the standard of all goodness.

The moral argument exposes the atheistic dilemma: if God does not exist, objective moral values cannot exist; yet moral values do exist; therefore, God exists. The existence of evil, far from disproving God, actually confirms Him, because evil presupposes an objective standard of good that only God provides. When the atheist calls something evil, he implicitly appeals to a transcendent moral law—one that cannot exist in a godless universe.

Christians, therefore, must demonstrate that moral truths flow from God's unchanging nature. His holiness defines what is good; His justice defines what is right. The gospel further reveals the only solution to man's moral guilt: the atoning death of Jesus Christ. The moral law drives us to the Savior, who alone can cleanse the conscience and restore fellowship with God.

Addressing Religious Pluralism

Religious pluralism, the idea that all religions are equally valid paths to God, is one of the most pervasive intellectual barriers in contemporary culture. It appeals to modern sensibilities of tolerance and inclusivity but contradicts the very essence of truth. Truth, by definition, is exclusive—if one worldview is true, opposing views must be false.

Jesus' declaration, "I am the way, and the truth, and the life; no one comes to the Father but through Me" (John 14:6), leaves no room for relativism. Christianity is not one truth among many but the only revelation of the true and living God. All other religions reflect man's attempt to reach God through human effort, while Christianity proclaims that God has reached down to man through Christ.

Pluralism also fails logically. The doctrines of the major religions contradict each other on fundamental issues: the nature of God, salvation, and the afterlife. They cannot all be true simultaneously. To claim that all religions are equally valid is to abandon the law of noncontradiction. The Christian faith alone provides a coherent explanation of sin, redemption, and the restoration of creation through the Messiah.

Christians must respond to pluralism not with arrogance but with conviction and compassion. The exclusivity of Christ is not narrow-mindedness but divine mercy. God has provided one sure way of salvation, and to reject it is to reject His love. The proclamation of the gospel is therefore the highest act of intellectual and moral honesty.

Faith as the Fulfillment of True Rationality

Faith and reason are not opposing forces; faith is the fulfillment of true rationality. Biblical faith is not blind belief but confident trust in the God who has revealed Himself through creation, Scripture, and Christ. The Christian believes because there is overwhelming evidence that God exists, that the Bible is His inspired Word, and that Jesus Christ rose from the dead.

Faith goes beyond reason but never against it. It acknowledges that reason alone cannot bridge the infinite gap between man and God. Faith receives divine truth where human reasoning reaches its limits. The harmony of faith and reason is evident throughout Scripture. Abraham believed God and acted upon that belief; Daniel reasoned from God's revealed truth in prayer; Paul appealed to evidence and logic before kings and philosophers. Christianity commands both heart and mind to love Jehovah completely (Matthew 22:37).

The intellectual life of the Christian is therefore one of continual renewal. Paul urged believers to be "transformed by the renewing of your mind" (Romans 12:2). This renewal occurs as the believer submits every thought to the authority of Scripture, allowing divine truth to shape reasoning, perception, and purpose. The Word of God provides the framework for all true knowledge.

When Christians encounter intellectual barriers—whether in philosophy, science, or culture—they must respond with the weapons of divine truth, not worldly speculation. Every argument raised against the knowledge of God must be dismantled by the power of Scripture and the illumination of the Holy Spirit. The gospel not only redeems the soul but also liberates the mind, restoring it to its proper function as an instrument of truth.

Through the wisdom of God's Word, the believer can confront the arrogance of human philosophy and demonstrate that only in Christ are "all the treasures of wisdom and knowledge hidden" (Colossians 2:3). True wisdom begins and ends with Him, for He alone is the source, the standard, and the goal of all truth.

Chapter 12 – The Assurance of Salvation

Main Verse: 1 John 5:13 – "These Things I Have Written to You Who Believe in the Name of the Son of God, so That You May Know That You Have Eternal Life."

The believer's confidence in salvation is not based on emotional fervor, mystical experience, or denominational affirmation, but upon the inspired and inerrant Word of God. The Apostle John, under the guidance of the Holy Spirit, wrote to give believers assurance—not presumption, not pride, but a biblically grounded certainty that comes from understanding Jehovah's purpose in Christ and the continuing responsibility of the believer to remain in faith, obedience, and sanctification.

The Basis of Assurance in Scripture

The foundation of assurance rests upon the reliability of Jehovah's promises and the sufficiency of Jesus Christ's atoning sacrifice. The Apostle John declared, "These things I have written to you who believe in the name of the Son of God, so that you may know that you have eternal life" (1 John 5:13). This statement affirms that assurance is based upon divine revelation, not subjective emotion. The believer's confidence is not self-generated; it arises from the testimony of Scripture that God's Word cannot fail.

Jehovah, through His inspired Word, assures the believer that salvation is both a present reality and a continuing path. Eternal life is not an abstract idea or a future hope only; it begins in this life as a relationship with the Father through the Son (John 17:3). However, this assurance does not negate the call to faithfulness. The Christian's confidence rests in what God has done, is doing, and will complete in those who "continue in the faith firmly established and steadfast" (Colossians 1:23).

The believer's assurance is not unconditional. It is conditional upon faith and obedience. The Holy Scriptures do not teach that one's initial act of faith eternally secures him regardless of his subsequent conduct. Rather, they teach that one must endure in faith until the end to be saved (Matthew 24:13). The pattern throughout Scripture reveals that salvation is a gift freely offered through grace, yet it is maintained through faithfulness to the covenant relationship initiated by Jehovah through His Son.

Faith Versus Feeling

The modern distortion of assurance often substitutes emotional experience for scriptural faith. Yet genuine faith is not a fleeting feeling but an informed conviction grounded in the Word of God.

The Apostle Paul wrote, "Faith comes from hearing, and hearing by the word of Christ" (Romans 10:17). This faith is rational, obedient, and persevering.

The Christian must never confuse the emotional elation of a religious experience with the true assurance of salvation. Feelings fluctuate; divine truth remains constant. A believer's confidence is anchored not in his own worthiness or in subjective experiences, but in the unchanging promises of Jehovah.

Faith that saves is a trusting reliance upon Christ's sacrificial work, leading to obedience. Hebrews 5:9 states that Jesus "became the source of eternal salvation to all who obey Him." Faith and obedience are inseparably linked. The kind of faith that produces salvation is a faith that demonstrates itself in action. James clarifies this in James 2:14, 26, emphasizing that "faith without works is dead." This does not mean that works earn salvation, but that genuine faith manifests itself in obedience to God's Word.

The believer who places faith in Christ alone, yet refuses to live in harmony with His commands, deceives himself. True assurance rests upon an active, living faith that results in works of righteousness—not as a means to merit salvation, but as evidence of the reality of one's faith.

Perseverance and Faithfulness

Scripture consistently teaches that salvation must be maintained through perseverance and continued obedience. Paul's exhortation to the Philippians makes this clear: "Work out your own salvation with fear and trembling" (Philippians 2:12). This admonition is not a call to self-salvation but an appeal to cooperate with God's saving purpose through faithful obedience. The believer must not be complacent but vigilant, recognizing that the Christian path involves continual spiritual growth and resistance to sin.

The principle of perseverance is further emphasized in passages such as Hebrews 10:26–27: "If we sin deliberately after receiving the knowledge of the truth, there no longer remains a sacrifice for sins." This solemn warning demonstrates that salvation can be forfeited through persistent disobedience and rejection of divine truth. The Israelites, though once delivered from Egypt, were later destroyed for unbelief (Jude 5). The same principle applies under the New Covenant. Salvation, though graciously given, requires endurance in faithfulness to Christ.

Jesus Himself said, "He who endures to the end will be saved" (Matthew 24:13). Thus, assurance does not eliminate the need for endurance; rather, true assurance strengthens the believer to remain steadfast under pressure. It is a living confidence that compels faithfulness.

Recognizing the Witness of the Word

The believer's assurance is confirmed by the witness of the inspired Scriptures. John affirms, "And the witness is this, that God has given us eternal life, and this life is in His Son" (1 John 5:11). The assurance of salvation rests in the objective testimony of God's Word, not in internal impressions or mystical experiences. The believer can know he possesses eternal life because the Word of Jehovah declares it so for those who continue in faith.

This witness is not a vague or mystical sensation within the heart, but the reliable testimony of the written Word. When Scripture declares that "whoever believes in the Son has eternal life" (John 3:36), that statement applies to the believer who continues to live by faith and obedience. It does not apply to one who abandons his faith or returns to the works of darkness.

The witness of the Word also exposes false assurance. Many presume salvation while walking in disobedience, but Jesus warned that not everyone who calls Him "Lord" will enter the Kingdom (Matthew 7:21–23). True assurance arises from a transformed life, consistent obedience, and a steadfast relationship with Jehovah through His Son.

Overcoming Spiritual Insecurity

Spiritual insecurity often arises when believers confuse their human imperfections with the forfeiture of salvation. Yet Scripture distinguishes between unintentional sins that result from human weakness and willful rebellion that leads to destruction. The believer's assurance remains intact when he sincerely repents and continues in faith, for "if we confess our sins, He is faithful and righteous to forgive us our sins and to cleanse us from all unrighteousness" (1 John 1:9).

However, one must not turn this promise into license for sin. The believer's security lies not in perpetual forgiveness without repentance, but in continual faithfulness and submission to God's moral will. The Christian who truly knows Jehovah will strive to walk in the light as He is in the light (1 John 1:7).

This balanced understanding frees the believer from both false security and crippling fear. False security deceives those who think salvation cannot be lost regardless of conduct; crippling fear paralyzes those who think salvation can be lost at any moment for minor failures. The truth lies in the middle: salvation is secure for those who continue in faith and obedience, but it is forfeited by deliberate apostasy or rebellion.

The assurance of salvation, therefore, is not static but dynamic. It grows stronger as the believer matures in faith, knowledge, and obedience. The believer is to "add to [his] faith virtue, and to virtue knowledge" (2 Peter 1:5), cultivating spiritual fruit that confirms his calling and election. Peter assures that "if you practice these things, you will never stumble" (2 Peter 1:10).

Living in the Confidence of Redemption

Living in assurance means walking daily in the light of redemption, confident not in one's own righteousness, but in Jehovah's mercy through Christ. The believer's confidence is not arrogance; it is humble certainty rooted in divine grace. Paul testified, "I know whom I have believed and am convinced that He is able to guard what I have entrusted to Him until that day" (2 Timothy 1:12).

This confidence motivates obedience and endurance. The believer who understands the seriousness of salvation will live in reverent gratitude, striving to please Jehovah in all things. The Christian life is not a passive acceptance of grace but an active participation in God's sanctifying purpose.

Eternal life is the ultimate reward for those who remain faithful until the end. The Scriptures make clear that while salvation begins with faith, it is consummated in perseverance. As Jesus said, "Be faithful until death, and I will give you the crown of life" (Revelation 2:10).

Salvation, therefore, is a journey—a path walked in continual dependence upon Jehovah's grace, guided by the truth of His Word, and sustained by obedient faith. The believer who abides in this path has every reason to be assured, for he walks not in presumption but in the light of divine promise.

Chapter 13 – The Church and the Defense of Faith

Main Verse: 1 Peter 3:15 – "Always Be Ready to Make a Defense to Everyone Who Asks You to Give an Account for the Hope That Is in You."

The Church is called not only to proclaim the gospel of salvation but also to preserve and defend it. Christianity is not a religion of blind belief; it is a faith grounded in reason, revelation, and history. The Apostle Peter's inspired exhortation in 1 Peter 3:15 commands believers to be ready to make a defense (Greek: *apologia*) to anyone who questions their hope in Christ. This verse forms the foundation of biblical apologetics—the rational defense of the Christian faith. It also underscores that every Christian, not merely the trained theologian or apologist, shares in this sacred duty.

The Church as the Pillar of Truth

In 1 Timothy 3:15, the Apostle Paul describes the congregation of believers as "the pillar and support of the truth." The Church is not the source of truth—Jehovah alone is the source—but it is the divinely appointed institution through which His truth is upheld, taught, and protected. The Church exists as the visible community of those sanctified through Christ and governed by Scripture. Its mission includes not only the proclamation of redemption but also the preservation of doctrinal purity against corruption.

The early Church faced relentless opposition from false teachers, pagan philosophies, and political powers hostile to truth. Yet it stood firm because its foundation was the Word of God, not the wisdom of men. Likewise, in every generation, the Church must remain the pillar of truth by holding fast to "the faith which was once for all delivered to the holy ones" (Jude 3). This demands fidelity to Scripture as the sole authority for faith and practice. Human traditions, philosophical reinterpretations, and modern cultural pressures must never be allowed to supplant the inspired Word.

The Church's identity as the pillar of truth obligates her to guard against theological compromise and moral decay. When the Church weakens in conviction, society loses its moral compass. When the Church stands firm in truth, even a hostile world must reckon with the light of divine revelation shining in its midst.

The Responsibility to Defend the Faith

The call to "make a defense" implies preparedness, courage, and clarity. The Greek term *apologia* conveys a reasoned argument made in response to questioning or challenge. Peter's instruction is not limited to public debate but extends to the personal witness of every believer. Each Christian must be equipped to explain what he believes, why he believes it, and how that belief transforms his life.

Defending the faith is not an act of hostility but of love. It flows from reverence for Christ as Lord in one's heart. The defense is to be offered "with gentleness and respect" (1 Peter 3:15), reflecting the character of the One we serve. Harshness and arrogance contradict the very gospel we proclaim. Yet gentleness does not mean compromise; it means presenting truth firmly, wisely, and compassionately.

The believer's defense of faith includes both offensive and defensive dimensions. Defensively, it involves exposing error, refuting false doctrine, and clarifying misconceptions about Scripture and salvation. Offensively, it includes proclaiming the truth persuasively, showing that the Christian worldview alone provides coherent answers to the deepest questions of human existence—origin, meaning, morality, and destiny.

Scripture calls every believer to be "a worker who does not need to be ashamed, accurately handling the word of truth" (2 Timothy 2:15). This requires study, reflection, and discipline. A believer who neglects the Word cannot effectively defend it. The Church must therefore cultivate intellectual and spiritual maturity among its members so that they can articulate the faith intelligently in a skeptical age.

Equipping the Congregation for Apologetics

For the Church to fulfill its role as defender of the faith, its members must be trained in sound doctrine and biblical reasoning. Apologetics is not reserved for theologians; it is a duty shared by all believers. Every Christian must understand the foundations of faith—the inspiration and inerrancy of Scripture, the nature of God, the deity of Christ, the reality of the resurrection, and the necessity of salvation through faith in Jesus alone.

Pastors and elders bear a solemn responsibility to equip the congregation for this task. Paul instructed Timothy to "preach the word; be ready in season and out of season; reprove, rebuke, exhort, with great patience and instruction" (2 Timothy 4:2). Sound teaching strengthens the Church's defense against deception. When the Church fails to teach doctrine and apologetics, it leaves its members vulnerable to the distortions of false religions, secular ideologies, and moral relativism.

The Church's teaching ministry must emphasize the sufficiency of Scripture as the final authority. The believer's defense must always proceed from the Word of God, not from human speculation. While logic and evidence can support faith, they must never replace divine revelation as the foundation of truth. The inspired Scriptures are fully capable of exposing error and establishing righteousness (2 Timothy 3:16–17).

Training in apologetics should therefore involve both the intellectual and spiritual dimensions. Knowledge must be joined with holiness. The most persuasive defense of the gospel comes not merely from eloquent reasoning but from a life that demonstrates the reality of redemption.

Unity and Discernment in Teaching

The Church must defend the faith while maintaining unity in truth. True unity is never achieved through compromise of doctrine but through shared submission to the authority of Scripture. The Apostle Paul admonished believers to "be of the same mind, maintaining the same love, united in spirit, intent on one purpose"

(Philippians 2:2). This purpose is the glorification of God through the faithful proclamation of His truth.

However, unity must not degenerate into uniformity of opinion on matters not essential to salvation. Christians may differ in secondary issues, but they must stand united on the essentials—the nature of God, the deity and humanity of Christ, salvation by grace through faith, the inspiration of Scripture, and the reality of resurrection and judgment.

Discernment is equally vital. The Church must test every teaching by the Word of God. The Bereans were commended because they examined the Scriptures daily to verify the apostolic message (Acts 17:11). Likewise, the modern Church must not be swayed by emotional appeals or popular movements that distort the gospel. Every sermon, every doctrine, and every ministry must be measured against the divine standard of Scripture.

False teachers, both ancient and modern, exploit ignorance and spiritual apathy. They twist the Scriptures to suit worldly desires. Therefore, discernment is not optional; it is essential for the survival of a faithful Church. Only by clinging to sound doctrine can the body of Christ remain pure and effective in its witness.

Evangelism as an Act of Reasonable Faith

True evangelism is inherently apologetic. The gospel calls for repentance and faith, but it also invites reasoned consideration. The Apostle Paul reasoned from the Scriptures, explaining and giving evidence that Jesus was the Christ (Acts 17:2–3). Evangelism involves proclaiming truth in such a way that the hearer is persuaded both intellectually and spiritually.

When believers engage the world, they must do so with clarity and conviction. The message of salvation through Jesus Christ stands upon historical and rational foundations—the fulfilled prophecies of Scripture, the eyewitness testimony of the resurrection, and the transformative power of the gospel in human lives. The Church must help believers to articulate these truths in language understandable to a skeptical audience.

Apologetic evangelism bridges the gap between truth and misunderstanding. It removes intellectual barriers that prevent people from hearing the gospel. Yet the goal of apologetics is not merely to win arguments but to win souls. The Christian defends the faith not for pride or personal triumph, but to bring others into a reconciled relationship with Jehovah through Christ.

The Church's Witness in a Skeptical World

The modern world is marked by skepticism, relativism, and moral confusion. Many reject the concept of absolute truth, preferring the shifting sands of subjective opinion. In such a climate, the Church's role as the pillar of truth becomes even more critical.

The Church must not retreat into silence or compromise but must boldly proclaim the exclusivity of Christ as the only way to salvation (John 14:6). The believer's defense of faith must therefore confront false worldviews—atheism, materialism, humanism, and religious pluralism—with the unchanging truth of Scripture.

The Church's witness must be visible both in doctrine and in conduct. The world must see in the Church a living testimony to the power of truth. Jesus declared that His followers are "the light of the world" (Matthew 5:14). That light must shine through uncompromising fidelity to Scripture and through the demonstration of love, humility, and holiness.

The defense of the faith, therefore, is not a task for scholars alone but the calling of the entire body of Christ. Each believer, through prayer, study, and obedience, contributes to the Church's collective witness in a world desperate for truth.

The Church that faithfully defends the gospel fulfills her divine purpose as the pillar of truth, the guardian of revelation, and the herald of salvation. In a time when truth is under relentless assault, the people of God must stand courageously upon the Word, ready to give a defense for the hope within them, proclaiming the gospel with clarity, compassion, and conviction until Christ returns.

Chapter 14 – Faith in a Postmodern World

Main Verse: Isaiah 5:20 – "Woe to those who call evil good, and good evil."

The Collapse of Absolute Truth in Modern Culture

The modern world has undergone a profound moral and intellectual transformation that has reshaped how truth itself is understood. Once, the idea of truth was regarded as fixed, objective, and rooted in divine revelation. Western civilization—especially in the centuries following the Protestant Reformation—stood upon the conviction that the Bible revealed immutable truth given by Jehovah, the Creator and Lawgiver of the universe. However, as secular humanism advanced through the Enlightenment, truth began to be redefined according to human perception rather than divine revelation. The late 20th and early 21st centuries have witnessed the full flowering of this philosophical rebellion against objective truth, known as postmodernism.

Postmodernism denies the existence of universal, objective truth. It asserts that reality is not discovered but constructed by individual or cultural interpretation. This mindset claims that what is "true" for one person may not be true for another, effectively placing human preference above divine revelation. In such a world, moral standards are no longer determined by the Creator's immutable law but are subject to shifting cultural moods, emotional reactions, or personal desires. As Isaiah's warning reminds us, this inversion of moral order—calling evil good and good evil—is not merely intellectual confusion; it is moral rebellion against Jehovah Himself.

The collapse of absolute truth has deeply affected every area of modern life. In education, students are taught that all viewpoints are equally valid, except those that claim exclusivity. In entertainment, morality is mocked as subjective and old-fashioned. In politics, justice is redefined by convenience or ideology rather than by righteousness. Even within some churches, biblical truth has been diluted by relativism, where Scripture is treated as symbolic or flexible rather than divinely authoritative. This is the tragedy of a postmodern world: the rejection of God's truth inevitably leads to confusion, corruption, and chaos.

Relativism's Assault on Faith

Relativism is the logical consequence of removing God as the source of truth. It claims that there are no moral absolutes, only perspectives. Yet the very claim "there is no absolute truth" is itself an absolute statement—a self-contradiction. This philosophical inconsistency reveals that relativism is not an intellectual position but a moral one. Humanity prefers moral autonomy to divine authority. In Romans 1:22, the Apostle Paul describes this same spirit of rebellion: "Claiming to be wise, they became fools."

Relativism erodes the foundation of faith because faith depends upon the trustworthiness of divine revelation. If truth is relative, then faith has no secure object. Belief becomes merely psychological comfort, not conviction grounded in reality. The authority of Scripture is then undermined, and the believer is tempted to reshape biblical teaching to suit cultural expectations. This is precisely what the enemy of truth desires. Satan's first recorded words in Scripture were an attack on the certainty of divine revelation: "Did God actually say...?" (Genesis 3:1). The same question echoes throughout postmodern philosophy.

In practice, relativism produces a society without moral direction. If good and evil are merely social constructs, then nothing can be condemned and nothing can be commended. The result is moral paralysis and the erosion of conscience. The prophet Amos lamented a similar time in Israel's history when truth was despised and justice perverted: "They hate him who reproves in the gate, and they abhor him who speaks the truth" (Amos 5:10). Today, those who speak the biblical truth about sin, morality, and salvation are branded as intolerant or hateful. Yet the Christian must recognize that the hostility of a relativistic world is the natural reaction of darkness to light (John 3:19–20).

The Christian Response to Moral Confusion

The believer must not retreat into silence or compromise. The confusion of the world is an opportunity for the Church to shine as a beacon of divine truth. Faith in a postmodern world requires conviction rooted in Scripture, not in personal feeling or cultural acceptance. As Paul exhorted Timothy, "Preach the word; be ready in season and out of season; reprove, rebuke, and exhort, with complete patience and teaching" (2 Timothy 4:2).

The Christian response to moral confusion must begin with renewed confidence in the authority and sufficiency of the Word of God. The Scriptures are not outdated cultural relics; they are the living, active Word of Jehovah (Hebrews 4:12). The truth revealed in the Bible transcends time, culture, and opinion because it originates from the eternal God who does not change (Malachi 3:6). When Christians build their worldview upon Scripture, they stand upon the same foundation that sustained the prophets, apostles, and faithful believers throughout history.

Furthermore, Christians must live in such a way that their conduct displays the beauty of divine truth. It is not enough to proclaim truth verbally; it must be embodied in the believer's character, speech, and actions. Jesus called His followers to be "the light of the world" (Matthew 5:14), which means illuminating a morally dark culture through godly living. In doing so, believers demonstrate that objective truth is not merely theoretical but transformative. The Word of God, applied faithfully, produces righteousness, wisdom, and peace that stand in contrast to the emptiness of relativism.

Truth as Objective and Divine

Truth exists because God exists. He is the ultimate source and standard of all that is true. Jesus Christ declared, "I am the way, and the truth, and the life" (John 14:6). This statement is absolute and exclusive. It affirms that truth is not a philosophical abstraction or a social construct; it is the very nature of the Son of God. Because Jehovah is immutable, His truth cannot evolve or contradict itself.

Psalm 119:160 affirms, "The sum of Your word is truth, and every one of Your righteous rules endures forever."

Objective truth is divine truth revealed to humanity through Scripture and through the person of Jesus Christ. It is not dependent upon human reasoning or cultural validation. The Christian worldview rests on the conviction that God has spoken, that His Word is reliable, and that His moral law is binding on all people for all time. Rejecting this truth leads to spiritual blindness, while receiving it leads to wisdom and life.

The postmodern rejection of objective truth is, at its core, a rejection of God's sovereignty. When people claim that truth is subjective, they are asserting their own autonomy against the Creator's authority. They elevate the self as the final arbiter of right and wrong, good and evil. Yet the Scripture warns that "there is a way that seems right to a man, but its end is the way to death" (Proverbs 14:12). True freedom and true wisdom are found only in submission to the divine truth revealed by Jehovah.

Restoring Biblical Certainty in the Mind

To resist the currents of postmodern confusion, believers must train their minds to think biblically. The Apostle Paul commands, "Do not be conformed to this world, but be transformed by the renewal of your mind" (Romans 12:2). This renewal is accomplished through the study, meditation, and application of Scripture. The Christian mind must be disciplined to evaluate all ideas, philosophies, and cultural trends through the lens of God's Word.

This intellectual restoration begins by affirming that the Bible is wholly trustworthy and fully sufficient. The Scriptures are "breathed out by God" (2 Timothy 3:16), meaning that they carry the very authority of the Creator. The believer who immerses his or her mind in the Word of God develops discernment—a spiritual clarity that can distinguish truth from deception. Hebrews 5:14 describes mature believers as those who "have their powers of discernment trained by constant practice to distinguish good from evil."

In a world intoxicated by subjectivity, Christians must recover confidence in propositional truth. The faith of the believer is not a vague feeling or mystical intuition but a rational commitment to the truth revealed by Jehovah. This conviction produces stability in an unstable world. As Jesus taught, those who hear His words and act upon them are like a house built on rock, immovable when storms arise (Matthew 7:24–25).

Standing Firm in a Confused Generation

Faithfulness in a postmodern world requires courage, conviction, and unwavering devotion to the truth. The believer must not be swayed by the pressures of cultural conformity or the fear of human disapproval. Instead, he or she must stand as a witness that truth is not determined by human vote but revealed by divine authority. Ephesians 6:13 exhorts Christians to "take up the whole armor of God... and having done all, to stand firm."

Standing firm involves more than intellectual agreement with biblical doctrines. It requires a life anchored in prayer, obedience, and evangelistic zeal. The Christian must proclaim the truth of Christ not only within the church but in every sphere of life—schools, workplaces, families, and public discourse. The world will accuse believers of arrogance for affirming absolute truth, but genuine humility lies in submission to God's revelation rather than surrender to cultural fashion.

In the midst of moral confusion, Jehovah's people must reflect His unchanging nature by living and speaking with clarity and compassion. Truth without love becomes harsh; love without truth becomes deceit. The faithful Christian balances both, proclaiming the truth in love as commanded in Ephesians 4:15.

The postmodern world may reject the concept of objective truth, but the believer knows that divine truth endures forever. Isaiah 40:8 declares, "The grass withers, the flower fades, but the word of our God will stand forever." Faith in a postmodern world is not blind belief against reason; it is confident trust in the God who cannot lie (Titus 1:2) and whose Word remains eternally reliable.

Through the power of the inspired Scriptures, Jehovah equips His people to discern error, to defend truth, and to demonstrate that faith rooted in divine revelation can withstand the collapse of every human philosophy. The Christian's calling is to remain steadfast—to know the truth, live the truth, and proclaim the truth until Christ returns and every falsehood is silenced before His glory.

Chapter 15 – Science and Scripture

Main Verse: Psalm 111:2 – "Great are the works of Jehovah; they are studied by all who delight in them."

Science as Discovery of God's Order

From the beginning of human history, Jehovah has revealed Himself as the Creator and Sustainer of an orderly universe. The psalmist's declaration that "great are the works of Jehovah" is both a theological affirmation and a call to scientific inquiry. When the inspired writer adds that these works "are studied by all who delight in them," he affirms that investigation into the natural world is not an act of rebellion against God but an act of worship and reverence toward Him.

Science, in its truest sense, is the systematic study of the works of Jehovah. It seeks to uncover the laws and patterns by which He governs His creation. This principle is evident from Genesis onward. When Jehovah formed the heavens and the earth, He established predictable cycles—the rising and setting of the sun, the seasons, and the renewal of life. These observable regularities form the foundation for all genuine scientific pursuit.

The ancient Hebrews were not ignorant of this order. In passages such as Genesis 8:22, Jehovah assures Noah, "While the earth remains, seedtime and harvest, cold and heat, summer and winter, day and night, shall not cease." Such consistency demonstrates that creation operates within fixed boundaries. The same uniformity that allows for agriculture also enables scientific discovery. The believer, therefore, sees the study of nature as a means of understanding Jehovah's faithfulness and majesty.

The scientific method, when properly used, mirrors the biblical principle of careful observation and rational inference. It is not a replacement for divine revelation but a tool for examining the world Jehovah made. The Christian who delights in the works of God recognizes that each new discovery, whether in astronomy, biology, or physics, further illuminates the wisdom of the Creator.

Misconceptions About Science and Faith Conflict

The modern claim that science and faith are in conflict is a misconception rooted not in fact but in philosophy. The supposed "warfare" between religion and science is largely a myth born out of materialistic and atheistic interpretations of scientific findings, not from the data themselves. Historically, many of the greatest scientific minds—such as Johannes Kepler, Isaac Newton, and Robert Boyle—were men of deep Christian faith who believed that studying nature was a way of glorifying Jehovah.

The biblical worldview provided the very foundation for modern science. It taught that the universe is rational because its Creator is rational, that nature follows laws because Jehovah is a God of order, and that humans can understand these laws because they are made in His image. Without these theological premises, science as we know it would have no reason to assume that the universe is intelligible.

The real conflict is not between science and Scripture but between materialism and theism. Materialism, the belief that all things arise from purely natural causes without any divine purpose, stands in direct opposition to the Bible's affirmation of Jehovah as the Creator. Yet when scientific findings are examined without bias, they align with the biblical testimony of design, order, and purpose in creation.

Misunderstandings also arise when Scripture is treated as a scientific textbook. The Bible was never intended to provide exhaustive explanations of physical mechanisms. Instead, it reveals the Who and Why of creation—Jehovah and His purpose—while allowing humanity to explore the How through observation and reasoning. Thus, faith and science complement one another rather than contradict.

The Biblical View of Creation

The first verse of the Bible establishes the foundation for all true knowledge: "In the beginning God created the heavens and the earth" (Genesis 1:1). The creation account is a literal and historical record that reveals Jehovah as the ultimate cause of all things. While the six "days" of creation are not necessarily 24-hour solar days, they represent six distinct periods of creative activity through which Jehovah progressively prepared the earth for human habitation.

This biblical framework refutes atheism, polytheism, and naturalism. It affirms that matter is not eternal, that the universe had a beginning, and that this beginning was the result of divine will. Modern cosmology, with its evidence of a finite universe originating from a single point, harmonizes with this revelation.

Genesis presents creation as a series of divine commands followed by immediate results. Each creative act concludes with the phrase, "and it was so," emphasizing the absolute authority of Jehovah's word. The narrative conveys both the power and intentionality of the Creator. He did not form the universe through random processes or evolutionary accidents but through purposeful design.

The creation of humankind in God's image (Genesis 1:26-27) sets humanity apart from all other living creatures. This likeness does not refer to physical appearance but to rational and moral capacity, the ability to reason, communicate, and exercise dominion under divine authority. The human mind, therefore, reflects the Creator's rational nature and makes the pursuit of science possible.

The Laws of Nature as Evidence of Divine Wisdom

The existence of consistent natural laws is one of the strongest evidences for the wisdom and constancy of Jehovah. Jeremiah 33:25 declares, "Thus says Jehovah: If I have not established My covenant with day and night and the fixed order of heaven and earth..." The prophet equates the stability of the universe with God's covenantal faithfulness. The regularity of nature, far from being an accident, is an expression of divine governance.

Every law of physics, chemistry, and biology points to an underlying intelligence. Gravity, electromagnetism, and the laws of thermodynamics demonstrate mathematical precision. The fine-tuning of universal constants—such as the speed of light, the gravitational constant, and the ratio of proton to electron mass—reveals delicate balances necessary for life. If any of these values were altered even slightly, the universe could not support life. Such precision is not the product of chance but of divine design.

The apostle Paul affirms this truth in Romans 1:20, writing, "For his invisible attributes, namely, his eternal power and divine nature, have been clearly perceived, ever since the creation of the world, in the things that have been made." The intricate order and harmony of the cosmos make Jehovah's existence undeniable to all honest observers.

The study of these laws is, therefore, not a departure from faith but a continuation of it. Every new discovery reveals a glimpse of Jehovah's mind. The believer who studies the sciences does so with humility, acknowledging that the more one learns about creation, the more one recognizes human limitations and the infinite wisdom of the Creator.

Refuting Materialistic Evolution

The theory of evolution, as commonly presented in materialistic terms, denies the necessity of a Creator and attributes life's complexity to unguided processes of chance and natural selection. This philosophy is not science but a worldview that excludes divine causation a priori. True science is based on observation and experimentation, but no scientist has ever observed life arising from non-living matter or one kind of organism evolving into another kind.

The fossil record does not demonstrate gradual transitions between major life forms. Instead, it shows the sudden appearance of fully formed species, followed by stability and extinction. This pattern is entirely consistent with the biblical account of creation, in which Jehovah made each kind to reproduce "according to its kind" (Genesis 1:24-25).

The complexity of biological systems further undermines evolutionary explanations. DNA, the molecule that carries genetic information, contains an intricate code that functions like language. Information, by definition, requires an intelligent source. Random mutations cannot generate new information on the scale necessary to produce the diversity of life observed today.

The human body, from the cellular level to the organ systems, reflects purposeful design. The interdependence of biological structures, such as the eye, ear, and circulatory system, demonstrates irreducible complexity—each part must function in coordination with others for the organism to survive. Such systems could not arise through incremental changes.

Moreover, the moral and spiritual nature of humanity cannot be explained through evolutionary processes. Conscience, creativity, and the capacity for worship point to a Creator who endowed man with His moral image. To reduce these capacities to biochemical reactions is to ignore their transcendence.

Evolution, as a materialistic philosophy, seeks to remove Jehovah from His rightful place as Creator. Yet the evidence from genetics, paleontology, and biochemistry continues to affirm design, order, and purpose—all attributes of divine creation. The Christian's confidence rests not in speculation but in revelation confirmed by observable reality.

How Science Strengthens Faith

Far from undermining belief in Jehovah, true science reinforces it. The more humanity learns about the universe, the more evident it becomes that creation reflects design and intelligence. Whether one looks through a telescope or a microscope, the complexity and beauty of the world point unmistakably to a Creator.

Scientific discovery often deepens the believer's awe of Jehovah's majesty. The vastness of space, with its billions of galaxies, reveals His power. The intricacies of the atom reveal His precision. The balance of ecosystems demonstrates His wisdom in sustaining life. These wonders lead the faithful to worship rather than doubt.

Faith does not reject evidence; it rightly interprets it through the lens of divine revelation. Psalm 19:1 declares, "The heavens declare the glory of God, and the sky above proclaims his handiwork." Every scientific observation is, in essence, an echo of that declaration. The Christian scientist, therefore, studies creation with the same reverence that the psalmist expressed in his worship.

Science also strengthens faith by reminding believers of Jehovah's faithfulness. The unchanging laws of nature reflect His unchanging character. Just as the sun rises each morning, so His promises remain sure. The predictability that makes science possible mirrors the reliability of the Creator's Word.

In the end, the harmony between science and Scripture is found not in blending theology with speculation but in recognizing that both nature and Scripture proceed from the same Author. The Bible reveals Jehovah's purpose; creation reveals His power. Together they form a unified testimony to His glory and truth.

Chapter 16 – When God Seems Silent

Main Verse: Psalm 13:1 – "How long, O Jehovah? Will You forget me forever?"

Biblical Examples of Divine Silence

Throughout Scripture, there are moments when Jehovah, though ever-present and all-knowing, chooses to remain silent toward His servants. This silence is not abandonment, nor is it disinterest; rather, it serves divine purposes that align perfectly with His wisdom and sovereignty. David's cry in Psalm 13:1 reflects the anguish of one who feels deserted: "How long, O Jehovah? Will You forget me forever? How long will You hide Your face from me?" Yet David's lament does not arise from disbelief but from faith seeking understanding. He knows Jehovah exists, hears, and cares. What he struggles with is the delay of divine intervention.

Job, likewise, experienced prolonged silence amid unbearable suffering. Though he cried out repeatedly, Jehovah withheld immediate response. Job 30:20 says, "I cry to You for help and You do not answer me; I stand, and You only look at me." Job's patience and faith were stretched, but Jehovah's silence did not mean rejection. In time, Jehovah spoke from the whirlwind, revealing His greatness and wisdom, humbling Job and refining his understanding.

Abraham endured divine silence between the promise and the fulfillment of Isaac's birth. From the moment Jehovah assured him that he would become a great nation, years of waiting followed, during which no voice or sign reaffirmed the promise. Yet "he did not waver in unbelief" (Romans 4:20), but trusted that God's timing was perfect.

Even our Lord Jesus experienced divine silence in the most intense moment of His suffering. Hanging upon the stake, He cried, "My God, My God, why have You forsaken Me?" (Matthew 27:46). Jehovah did not rescue Him from death, yet that silence accomplished humanity's redemption. The silence of the Father was not a sign of indifference but the fulfillment of divine justice and mercy.

Thus, from David to Job, from Abraham to Christ, divine silence is never arbitrary. It is purposeful, refining, and deeply rooted in Jehovah's redemptive plan.

Testing of Faith Through Waiting

Jehovah often tests His servants not through immediate answers but through waiting. Faith is not proven by receiving quick responses but by steadfast trust when heaven appears still. Waiting reveals the depth of belief and exposes whether trust depends upon circumstances or upon God's unchanging character.

In Deuteronomy 8:2–3, Moses reminded Israel that Jehovah allowed them to hunger in the wilderness "to humble you and to test you, to know what was in your heart, whether you would keep His commandments or not." The silence of provision was designed to teach them that "man does not live by bread alone, but man lives by everything that proceeds out of the mouth of Jehovah." Silence became the classroom of faith.

The apostle Peter later explained that faith is refined "by fire" so that it "may be found to result in praise and glory and honor at the revelation of Jesus Christ" (1 Peter 1:7). A faith that endures silence is a faith not dependent upon sight. Silence reveals whether one's confidence lies in Jehovah Himself or merely in His gifts.

When believers cry out and no immediate response comes, they stand at the crossroad between despair and trust. Those who choose trust discover that waiting itself becomes the act of worship. The Psalmist later wrote, "I waited patiently for Jehovah; and He inclined to me and heard my cry" (Psalm 40:1). Notice that the act of waiting did not precede Jehovah's attention—it was itself the process through which the heart was shaped to perceive His mercy.

The Growth of Spiritual Patience

Patience is not passivity but perseverance shaped by faith. Divine silence is one of the primary means by which Jehovah cultivates this virtue within His people. James 1:3–4 teaches, "The testing of your faith produces endurance. And let endurance have its perfect result, that you may be perfect and complete, lacking in nothing."

The believer who experiences silence learns to depend less on emotional assurance and more on the unchanging promises of

Scripture. Jehovah's silence does not contradict His Word; rather, it confirms that His Word is sufficient even when His voice is withheld. As the believer meditates upon the written Word, the heart finds strength to endure without complaint.

Consider Hannah in 1 Samuel 1. For years she prayed for a child, yet heaven was silent. Her rival provoked her, and her soul grew weary. But through years of quiet anguish, her faith deepened until she prayed with complete surrender, promising that her son would belong wholly to Jehovah. The silence shaped her heart, and when Jehovah finally responded, she recognized that the delay had not been neglect but preparation.

Spiritual patience transforms anxiety into endurance and despair into disciplined hope. It teaches the believer to interpret silence not as divine distance but as divine craftsmanship. Jehovah molds His servants through waiting so that their confidence is built upon His character rather than His immediate activity.

Understanding God's Timing and Sovereignty

Jehovah's timing operates beyond human perception. Ecclesiastes 3:11 declares, "He has made everything beautiful in its time." The apparent delay of divine response often stems from our limited view of time and purpose. What seems like postponement to man is precision in the eyes of God.

Jehovah is never hurried nor hindered. His sovereignty means that every delay, silence, or pause fits into His perfect orchestration of events. He who sees the end from the beginning cannot act too soon or too late. The silence of God often prepares the way for a greater revelation of His power and faithfulness.

In John 11, when Jesus learned that Lazarus was sick, He deliberately remained where He was for two more days. This silence and delay resulted in a greater display of divine glory when Lazarus was raised from the dead. Had Jesus gone immediately, Lazarus would have been healed—but through waiting, many came to believe that He was the resurrection and the life.

Jehovah's silence often conceals His greatest work in progress. What appears as inactivity is often divine alignment—circumstances being arranged for the manifestation of His will. When His timing arrives, it becomes evident that His silence was not absence but preparation. The believer's task is to remain still and know that He is God (Psalm 46:10).

Prayer in the Midst of Silence

When Jehovah seems silent, prayer must not cease. The faithful response to silence is not withdrawal but persistence. Jesus taught, "that at all times they ought to pray and not to lose heart" (Luke 18:1). The parable of the persistent widow illustrates that continual prayer demonstrates trust in Jehovah's justice and timing.

David, though feeling forgotten, continued to pray. Psalm 13 itself begins in lament but ends in praise: "But I have trusted in Your lovingkindness; my heart shall rejoice in Your salvation. I will sing to Jehovah, because He has dealt bountifully with me." Between despair and rejoicing lies the turning point of continued prayer.

In the midst of silence, prayer becomes less about seeking answers and more about maintaining fellowship. Even when Jehovah does not speak, the believer can still speak to Him. This ongoing communion fortifies the heart against bitterness and unbelief.

Philippians 4:6–7 instructs, "Be anxious for nothing, but in everything by prayer and supplication with thanksgiving let your requests be made known to God. And the peace of God, which surpasses all comprehension, will guard your hearts and your minds in Christ Jesus." Prayer does not always change circumstances immediately, but it changes the believer's disposition within them.

The Holy Scriptures never portray prayer as a mechanism to manipulate God's hand but as a means to align the believer's heart with His will. Silence teaches believers to seek the Giver more than the gift, the presence more than the provision. Persistent prayer during silence transforms impatience into intimacy.

Trusting in the Character of Jehovah

When explanations are withheld, the believer must rest in the unchanging character of Jehovah. His silence never contradicts His nature. He remains righteous, faithful, loving, and wise. Malachi 3:6 affirms, "For I, Jehovah, do not change." Thus, even when His voice is unheard, His heart toward His people remains steadfast.

David's movement from anguish to assurance in Psalm 13 demonstrates this truth. Though he began in sorrow, he concluded in trust: "I have trusted in Your lovingkindness." The Hebrew term for lovingkindness, *chesed*, denotes covenantal loyalty. Jehovah's silence never breaks covenant; it tests whether His servants will cling to that covenantal loyalty even when sight and sound fail.

Isaiah 50:10 provides a fitting summary: "Who is among you that fears Jehovah, that obeys the voice of His servant, that walks in darkness and has no light? Let him trust in the name of Jehovah and rely on his God." To walk in darkness without light means to continue in obedience even when no divine confirmation is perceived. Trusting in the name of Jehovah is to rely upon His revealed character—the assurance that He is good, just, and true.

Silence, therefore, is not divine neglect but divine invitation. Jehovah calls His children to trust not in sensory reassurance but in the certainty of His person. Faith, in its purest form, believes even when unseen and unheard.

The believer who endures silence emerges with a deeper, purified faith. The waiting soul discovers that Jehovah was never absent—He was near, shaping the heart for greater usefulness and maturity. As Psalm 37:7 exhorts, "Rest in Jehovah and wait patiently for Him." Those who learn this rest find that silence, rather than diminishing their faith, becomes the crucible in which it is perfected.

Chapter 17 – The Discipline of Faith

Main Verse: 2 Corinthians 5:7 – "For we walk by faith, not by sight."

Faith as a Lifelong Journey

The Christian life is not a brief experience of spiritual awakening but a lifelong discipline grounded in faith. The Apostle Paul's declaration, "For we walk by faith, not by sight," defines the essence of this journey (2 Corinthians 5:7). Faith, in its biblical sense, is not a mere emotional feeling or intellectual assent; it is the constant reliance upon Jehovah's promises through Christ, anchored in His revealed Word. Faith is a continuing movement toward deeper trust, where the believer learns to lean upon what is unseen and eternal rather than upon the visible and transient.

The initial act of faith at conversion begins a process of sanctification in which the believer's confidence in Jehovah matures through constant exercise. Hebrews 11:1 describes faith as "the assurance of things hoped for, the conviction of things not seen." The believer's assurance grows as he acts upon God's Word and experiences its faithfulness. This walk by faith is a discipline—an intentional cultivation of spiritual perception that transcends the sensory evidence of the world. The faithful one must train his heart to trust God's character and promises even when physical sight offers no evidence of fulfillment.

Faith is thus a journey of submission to Jehovah's sovereignty. Abraham serves as the archetype of this journey. When he was called to leave his homeland, "he went out, not knowing where he was going" (Hebrews 11:8). His obedience sprang from faith, and his faith was sustained through obedience. The believer today is called to the same pattern—a continual progression of trust, surrender, and obedience that reflects steadfast devotion to the One who cannot lie. Faith's journey extends beyond initial belief to daily living, demanding that each step be taken in alignment with God's revealed will.

The Role of Obedience in Strengthening Faith

True faith cannot be separated from obedience. The Epistle of James emphasizes that "faith without works is dead" (James 2:26). This is not to suggest that salvation is earned by works, but rather that genuine faith inevitably produces obedience. Faith is strengthened when it is tested through action. Each act of obedience reinforces trust in Jehovah's reliability and deepens spiritual confidence in His Word.

Obedience demonstrates that the believer acknowledges God's authority over his life. Jesus Himself said, "If you love Me, you will keep My commandments" (John 14:15). Faith that does not manifest itself in obedience is theoretical, not transformative. The faithful believer learns to obey even when the reasons for obedience are not immediately visible. This pattern mirrors the obedience of Noah, who "by faith... prepared an ark for the salvation of his household" (Hebrews 11:7). His obedience was not based on empirical evidence of a coming flood but upon Jehovah's spoken Word.

Obedience requires humility. It demands the submission of human reasoning to divine revelation. Faith grows stronger when the believer chooses to act upon what God has declared rather than what seems rational or convenient. Each decision of obedience reinforces the believer's spiritual discipline, training his heart to trust the unseen realities of God's kingdom. This continual pattern of hearing, believing, and obeying establishes the believer in righteousness and produces spiritual steadfastness.

Thus, obedience is both the fruit and the fortifier of faith. Through it, the believer learns to discern the voice of God in Scripture and to respond without hesitation. The discipline of faith, therefore, is never idle. It compels action, submission, and trust that lead to maturity in Christ.

Perseverance Through Adversity

Faith is most vividly refined in adversity. The Apostle Peter wrote, "so that the proof of your faith, being more precious than gold which perishes though tested by fire, may be found to result in praise and glory and honor at the revelation of Jesus Christ" (1 Peter 1:7). Trials are not designed to destroy faith but to purify it, stripping away reliance upon worldly securities and deepening dependence upon Jehovah.

Adversity exposes the genuineness of faith. When difficulties arise, the believer is forced to decide whether his confidence rests in visible circumstances or in the unchanging Word of God. The faithful one perseveres, not by his own strength, but by drawing upon divine grace. The Apostle Paul expressed this truth in his own life, declaring, "when I am weak, then I am strong" (2 Corinthians 12:10). Faith thrives when the believer acknowledges his weakness and relies wholly on Jehovah's sustaining power.

This perseverance is not passive endurance but active trust. It requires that the believer continue to obey, pray, and meditate upon Scripture even when comfort is absent. Faith's discipline demands persistence in righteousness, knowing that Jehovah's purposes are accomplished through the testing of belief. Adversity is the furnace in which faith is purified, producing endurance and character (Romans 5:3–4).

The believer who endures hardship with unwavering trust honors Jehovah more profoundly than one who follows Him only in prosperity. Such faith is disciplined, tested, and proven. It reflects an eternal perspective—seeing beyond temporary affliction to the promised glory that awaits those who remain steadfast in their devotion.

The Renewal of the Mind Through Scripture

The discipline of faith cannot flourish apart from the renewal of the mind through God's Word. Romans 12:2 commands, "Do not be conformed to this world, but be transformed by the renewing of your mind." Faith grows in proportion to the believer's engagement with Scripture, for "faith comes from hearing, and hearing through the word of Christ" (Romans 10:17).

Renewal of the mind means reorienting one's thinking from human reasoning to divine revelation. The believer must discipline his thoughts, filtering every idea, emotion, and decision through the lens of Scripture. The Bible is not merely a devotional text but the living voice of Jehovah, through which He instructs, corrects, and strengthens His people. The disciplined Christian studies it not only to gain knowledge but to align his will with God's will.

This renewal transforms perception. The believer begins to interpret life through spiritual truth rather than through worldly logic. As the mind is saturated with Scripture, faith becomes increasingly stable, no longer swayed by emotional impulses or societal pressure. This mental transformation guards the believer against spiritual deception and cultivates discernment. The Holy Spirit, through the Word, reshapes desires, priorities, and attitudes, producing the fruit of righteousness in daily living.

The discipline of faith therefore requires daily immersion in the Word of God. Prayerful study, meditation, and obedience to biblical principles form the foundation of a mature and enduring trust in Jehovah. Without such renewal, faith becomes vulnerable to doubt and compromise. The believer's mind must continually be cleansed and refocused, ensuring that his confidence rests solely upon divine truth.

Faith Expressed in Daily Choices

Faith is not an abstract principle; it manifests itself in the ordinary choices of everyday life. The believer who walks by faith demonstrates his trust in Jehovah through consistent decisions that reflect godly priorities. Whether in work, relationships, stewardship, or moral conduct, each choice becomes an opportunity to affirm belief in God's sovereignty.

Faith guides how the Christian uses his time, resources, and influence. The faithful one prioritizes obedience to God over the pursuit of worldly comfort. Jesus taught, "Seek first the kingdom of God and his righteousness, and all these things will be added to you" (Matthew 6:33). This command reflects the heart of faith—a willingness to trust God's provision and direction in every circumstance.

Walking by faith requires moral courage. It demands that the believer uphold truth when falsehood is popular and practice righteousness when compromise seems easier. Every act of integrity becomes a testimony of faith. The disciplined believer refuses to be shaped by worldly values or fear of human opinion. Instead, he measures his conduct by Scripture, trusting that Jehovah rewards those who diligently seek Him (Hebrews 11:6).

Faith is expressed not only in great acts of devotion but also in small, consistent choices. The believer's speech, attitudes, and reactions must all reflect his confidence in God's promises. In every aspect of life, faith directs behavior toward godly living. The daily practice of faith builds spiritual resilience and deepens one's communion with Jehovah. Through disciplined living, faith becomes visible, tangible, and influential.

Becoming Mature in Spiritual Conviction

The ultimate goal of the discipline of faith is maturity in spiritual conviction. Spiritual maturity is not measured by knowledge alone but by steadfast trust and obedience under all conditions. The Apostle Paul exhorted believers to "be steadfast, immovable, always abounding in the work of the Lord" (1 Corinthians 15:58). Such firmness of conviction results from a lifetime of walking by faith and not by sight.

Mature faith is unshaken by doubt, fear, or worldly temptation. It has learned, through experience, that Jehovah's Word is absolutely reliable. The mature believer does not rely on fluctuating emotions but on the constancy of divine truth. His convictions are rooted deeply in Scripture and sustained by continual communion with God through prayer and study.

This maturity produces spiritual discernment—the ability to distinguish between truth and error, righteousness and sin. Hebrews 5:14 explains that "solid food is for the mature, who because of practice have their senses trained to discern good and evil." The disciplined believer grows in this discernment as he consistently applies God's Word to his life.

Faith's maturity results in unwavering peace and confidence. The believer who has cultivated disciplined faith does not panic in uncertainty nor falter under pressure. His life reflects the stability of one who trusts fully in Jehovah's sovereignty. Through this maturity, he becomes a witness to others, demonstrating the reality and power of faith that is anchored in divine truth.

The discipline of faith, therefore, is the process by which believers are conformed to the likeness of Christ. It is a journey of learning to trust, obey, persevere, renew the mind, and live daily in the confidence of God's promises. Those who walk this path experience the profound joy of resting in Jehovah's faithfulness, assured that "the righteous one will live by faith" (Romans 1:17).

Chapter 18 – The Power of Testimony

Main Verse: Revelation 12:11 – "And they overcame him because of the blood of the Lamb and because of the word of their testimony."

Personal Testimony as a Witness of Truth

The book of Revelation unveils the great spiritual conflict between Jehovah and Satan, a conflict that has raged since Eden. In Revelation 12:11, the inspired writer John records how faithful believers "overcame him because of the blood of the Lamb and because of the word of their testimony." The "him" in this verse refers to Satan, the accuser of the brothers, whose strategy has always been deceit, intimidation, and accusation. Yet the followers of Christ triumphed—not by worldly means, but through two unshakable powers: the atoning blood of Jesus Christ and their courageous proclamation of truth.

The testimony of a believer is not a mere recollection of personal experiences but a declaration of Jehovah's transforming grace and power through His Son. It is a witness to divine truth, anchored in the revelation of Scripture and confirmed by a life that has been changed. The "word of their testimony" points to a verbal confession that flows from a regenerated heart—a life visibly marked by repentance, faith, and obedience. This kind of testimony exalts not the person, but the Redeemer.

A genuine personal testimony stands as evidence before the world that Jehovah's Word is living and active. When a believer shares how Christ brought him from spiritual death to life, from darkness to light, it gives tangible proof of the gospel's power. This is not an appeal to emotion but to truth. Testimony serves as a personal witness that validates the authority of the Scriptures and the reality of the new birth. As the Apostle John wrote elsewhere, "We proclaim to you what we have seen and heard, so that you also may have fellowship with us" (1 John 1:3). Testimony invites others into that same fellowship—into reconciliation with God through Christ.

The Early Christians as Models of Courage

The early Christians embodied the very essence of this verse. In a hostile world ruled by Rome, they faced imprisonment, exile, and execution for refusing to renounce their allegiance to Christ. Yet, rather than silencing them, persecution only amplified their testimony. Their courage was not the product of human strength but of divine conviction. They had encountered the risen Christ and could not deny what they knew to be true.

From Stephen, who testified before the Sanhedrin even as stones struck him, to Paul, who boldly proclaimed Christ before governors and kings, their testimonies carried the fragrance of faithfulness. These early witnesses understood that their lives were not their own; they belonged to the One who purchased them with His blood. Their testimony was therefore both confession and commission—a confession of truth and a commission to proclaim it regardless of cost.

Their courage continues to inspire believers today. The early Christians remind us that true testimony cannot coexist with compromise. Their boldness sprang from conviction, not convenience. When they confessed "Jesus is Lord," they defied the idols of their age. Likewise, believers today must not be silent before a culture hostile to biblical truth. The testimony of Christ's followers remains the greatest refutation of unbelief and the most powerful defense of the gospel's authenticity.

The Transforming Evidence of Regeneration

At the heart of testimony is transformation. Regeneration is the divine act by which Jehovah imparts new spiritual life to one who was dead in trespasses and sins. This change is not merely moral or emotional but spiritual and radical. The person who once lived in rebellion against God is made alive by His grace and power through the sacrifice of Christ.

When Paul wrote to the Corinthians, he reminded them, "If anyone is in Christ, he is a new creation; the old things have passed away; behold, new things have come" (2 Corinthians 5:17). This is not a figure of speech but a literal reality. The believer's heart, desires, and affections are transformed. Sin no longer reigns; righteousness becomes the new pursuit.

The testimony of regeneration, therefore, is more than words. It is seen in the fruit of repentance, the pursuit of holiness, and the steadfast commitment to Jehovah's will. The believer's life becomes living evidence that Christ still changes lives. This transformation cannot be explained by natural means; it is the work of the Holy Spirit through the power of God's Word.

Every regenerated believer becomes a witness that Jesus Christ truly saves, forgives, and restores. This is why the "word of their testimony" carried such weight. It was not theory but reality. It was the testimony of men and women whose lives bore irrefutable evidence of Jehovah's grace.

Testifying with Humility and Conviction

Faithful testimony is not an act of pride but of humility. To testify of Christ is to confess one's utter dependence upon Him. A believer speaks, not to glorify self, but to magnify the Savior. True testimony begins with the recognition that all glory belongs to Jehovah and that every spiritual victory is the result of His mercy.

The Apostle Paul, though one of the greatest witnesses in history, consistently spoke of himself as the least of the apostles and unworthy of his calling. His testimony always centered upon Christ—"We preach not ourselves, but Jesus Christ as Lord" (2 Corinthians 4:5). Likewise, when a believer shares his testimony, he is to do so with the same spirit of humility, remembering that salvation is not earned by works but received by grace.

Yet humility must never weaken conviction. A timid or vague testimony dishonors the truth it seeks to proclaim. Conviction gives testimony its authority, for it springs from a settled assurance that God's Word is true. The believer who has experienced forgiveness and transformation cannot remain silent. As Peter declared before the rulers of his day, "We cannot stop speaking about what we have seen and heard" (Acts 4:20).

Humility guards against self-exaltation, while conviction preserves faithfulness to truth. Together they produce a testimony that honors Christ and draws others toward repentance.

Overcoming Fear Through Faithful Witness

Fear has always been one of Satan's chief weapons against those who would testify of Christ. He whispers threats of rejection, ridicule, or loss to silence the believer's voice. Yet Revelation 12:11 reveals how the faithful overcame him: through the blood of the Lamb and the word of their testimony. The blood of the Lamb represents redemption—Christ's victory over sin and death. The word of their testimony represents the believer's active participation in that victory through public confession.

When a Christian testifies, he declares allegiance to the conquering Christ and renounces the dominion of Satan. This act of witness disarms fear because it rests on divine authority, not human courage. The believer testifies not in his own strength but in the confidence that Christ is with him. As Jesus said, "Whoever confesses Me before men, him I will also confess before My Father who is in heaven" (Matthew 10:32).

Faithful witness transforms fear into faith. It strengthens the believer and encourages others. When a Christian stands firm and speaks truthfully about Christ's work in his life, he participates in the ongoing triumph of the Lamb over the accuser. The enemy's power is broken not through human argument but through steadfast obedience and testimony that glorifies Jehovah.

The Eternal Reward of the Faithful

The testimony of the saints is not forgotten. Those who overcome through faith and perseverance are promised an eternal reward. Their victory is sealed in the blood of the Lamb, and their faithfulness will be acknowledged in the presence of God. The book of Revelation later describes these faithful ones as those who "follow the Lamb wherever He goes" (Revelation 14:4).

Their reward is not earthly fame but everlasting fellowship with Christ. They will share in His triumph and reign with Him in His Kingdom. Their testimony, once despised by the world, will stand as everlasting proof of Jehovah's righteousness and justice.

Every believer who bears witness to Christ's truth participates in that same eternal victory. The act of testifying is not only a present duty but also an investment in eternal glory. As Paul reminded Timothy, "If we endure, we will also reign with Him" (2 Timothy 2:12). Those who hold fast their confession, even in the face of persecution or death, demonstrate the unshakable power of faith rooted in truth.

In the final triumph of the redeemed, the testimony of each believer will echo as part of the great chorus of victory—a witness that the Lamb's blood has conquered all evil and that truth has prevailed forever.

Chapter 19 – Faith That Endures

Main Verse: Hebrews 10:23 – "Let us hold fast the confession of our hope without wavering, for He who promised is faithful."

The Endurance of True Belief

Faith that endures is not a mere emotional attachment to religious ideas or fleeting expressions of devotion during favorable circumstances. It is a steadfast confidence grounded in the truth of God's Word, anchored in the unchangeable character of Jehovah, who never fails to fulfill His promises. The writer of Hebrews urges believers to "hold fast the confession of our hope without wavering," because the endurance of genuine faith depends not upon human strength but upon the unwavering faithfulness of Jehovah Himself. This perseverance is not a natural quality but a spiritual discipline cultivated through continual reliance on God's promises and the transforming power of His inspired Word.

True faith is not passive belief; it is active trust expressed through consistent obedience, even when human reasoning or external conditions seem unfavorable. Such faith acknowledges that Jehovah has the sovereign right to direct all things in harmony with His purpose. The endurance of faith, therefore, is rooted in an intimate relationship with God through His Son, Jesus Christ, who is both the "author and perfecter of our faith" (Hebrews 12:2). Christ's example of obedience unto death demonstrates that faith's endurance is sustained by absolute trust in the Father's goodness and justice, not by an expectation of earthly ease.

Faith that endures perseveres through human imperfection, opposition, and uncertainty because it rests on Jehovah's unchangeable Word. The believer's strength comes from Scripture, prayer, and the fellowship of fellow Christians who mutually encourage steadfastness. As 1 John 5:4 explains, "This is the victory that has overcome the world—our faith." Enduring faith triumphs because it is not self-generated; it draws its vitality from the living God who cannot lie (Titus 1:2).

Standing Firm Amid Opposition

From the earliest days of the Christian congregation, believers have faced hostility for their allegiance to Christ. The exhortation to "hold fast" in Hebrews 10:23 was written to a community that suffered public reproach, loss of property, and threats to life because of their faith (Hebrews 10:32–34). The call to stand firm amid opposition was not an abstract idea but a command anchored in the reality that persecution was a natural outcome of faithful discipleship. Jesus Himself warned that "if they persecuted Me, they will also persecute you" (John 15:20). Faith that endures does not crumble under societal rejection but remains loyal to Jehovah's standards despite cost or consequence.

Endurance is not achieved through human willpower or self-reliance; rather, it comes from maintaining spiritual focus on Jehovah's promises. Believers stand firm because they recognize that their trials are not divine punishments or "tests" imposed by God, but the natural result of living in a world alienated from righteousness. The hostility of the world arises from Satan's opposition to Jehovah's sovereignty, and faithful Christians inevitably face the brunt of that resistance. Yet even in such times, Jehovah's Word assures His people that "He will not let you be tempted beyond what you can bear, but will also provide the way out so that you can endure it" (1 Corinthians 10:13). This endurance, therefore, is not stoic resignation but confident perseverance through divine guidance.

Christians are called to be steadfast because their loyalty to Jehovah demonstrates that truth and righteousness cannot be extinguished by the pressures of this world. The apostle Peter urged believers to resist the Devil, "firm in the faith," knowing that "the same sufferings are being experienced by your brotherhood in the world" (1 Peter 5:9). Standing firm is both a testimony of faith and a witness to others that Jehovah's power is greater than any human or demonic opposition.

The Role of Hope in Persevering Faith

Hope is the sustaining force that enables faith to endure. The hope referred to in Hebrews 10:23 is not wishful thinking but confident expectation based on the promises of God, who "cannot lie" (Titus 1:2). Hope gives direction to faith, enabling believers to persevere even when present circumstances are discouraging. Without hope, faith weakens; but with hope firmly fixed on Jehovah's future restoration through Christ's Kingdom, the believer's confidence remains secure.

The Christian hope encompasses both heavenly and earthly promises. A select group of faithful ones will rule with Christ in the heavens, while the majority of obedient mankind will inherit eternal life on a restored earth (Psalm 37:29; Revelation 21:3–4). This expectation motivates perseverance because it reminds believers that their sufferings are temporary and that Jehovah's purposes will ultimately prevail. The apostle Paul wrote, "For I consider that the sufferings of this present time are not worth comparing with the glory that will be revealed in us" (Romans 8:18). Hope transforms endurance from mere survival into joyful anticipation.

Hope also guards against spiritual fatigue. When faith encounters discouragement, hope renews the believer's focus on the promises that lie ahead. It reminds the Christian that God's timetable is perfect and that His fulfillment of promises is certain, even if delayed from a human perspective. As Hebrews 6:19 declares, "We have this hope as an anchor for the soul, both sure and firm." Thus, enduring faith and steadfast hope operate together, sustaining the believer through all of life's imperfections.

Encouragement from the Cloud of Witnesses

The "cloud of witnesses" described in Hebrews 12:1 refers to the faithful men and women of earlier times whose lives demonstrate the reality of faith. Abel, Enoch, Noah, Abraham, Sarah, Moses, and others lived by faith even when they did not see the complete fulfillment of Jehovah's promises in their lifetimes (Hebrews 11:1–40). Their endurance testifies that genuine faith does not depend upon immediate results but trusts God's Word absolutely.

The example of these witnesses encourages modern believers to "run with endurance the race that is set before us" (Hebrews 12:1). Their faith was not passive belief but active obedience under difficult circumstances. Noah faced ridicule for constructing the ark in a corrupt world; Abraham left his homeland without knowing his destination; Moses chose to share the sufferings of God's people rather than enjoy the temporary pleasures of Egypt. Each of these individuals demonstrated that faith endures not because of favorable conditions but because of unwavering trust in Jehovah's promises.

Their stories also remind us that endurance is not an unattainable virtue reserved for ancient heroes. The same God who sustained them provides believers today with His inspired Word to strengthen their conviction. The Scriptures stand as both a record of God's faithfulness and a source of courage for every generation. As Romans 15:4 assures, "Whatever was written in former times was written for our instruction, so that through endurance and the comfort from the Scriptures we might have hope." Thus, the "cloud of witnesses" continues to inspire faith that perseveres until the realization of all divine promises.

Faith Tested in Persecution (God Does Not Test Us)

It is crucial to distinguish between faith being *proven* through circumstances and faith being *tested* by God. Jehovah never instigates evil or imposes hardship to assess the faith of His people. James 1:13 states unequivocally, "When under trial, let no one say, 'I am being tried by God,' for with evil things God cannot be tried nor does He himself try anyone." This verse establishes a clear theological principle: Jehovah is wholly righteous and cannot be the source of evil or temptation. Therefore, the notion that God deliberately "tests" His servants through pain or loss misrepresents His nature.

Human suffering results from three primary sources: human imperfection, satanic influence, and the consequences of living in a fallen world. Lamentations 3:38 affirms, "From the mouth of the

Most High bad things and what is good do not go forth." Evil, therefore, arises not from divine orchestration but from the misuse of human free will. James 1:14–15 explains that each person is "enticed by his own desires" and that sin, once fully developed, "brings forth death." Jehovah allows such circumstances to exist because He has granted humanity the dignity of free will, yet He never causes the evils that afflict mankind.

While God permits adversity as part of the human condition, He remains the provider of strength, wisdom, and comfort to those who turn to Him. James 1:5 promises that "if any of you lacks wisdom, let him ask of God, who gives generously to all without reproach." Thus, when believers experience difficulty, their endurance is supported not because God is testing them but because He equips them through His Word to overcome. Jehovah's guidance helps His people to mature spiritually without ever resorting to evil as an instrument of instruction. Faith in persecution, then, is refined by obedience to Scripture and reliance on divine wisdom, never by attributing hardship to God's will.

To suggest that Jehovah sends calamity to purify faith contradicts His revealed character. Psalm 145:17 declares, "Jehovah is righteous in all His ways," and Deuteronomy 32:4 confirms, "All His ways are justice." These passages affirm that everything God does is consistent with His holiness and goodness. Evil cannot originate from Him, and He takes no delight in human suffering. Instead, He provides His Word as the means by which faith is strengthened, giving believers the tools to endure the consequences of a sinful world without losing trust in His righteousness.

Awaiting the Fulfillment of Jehovah's Promises

Enduring faith ultimately looks beyond present conditions to the fulfillment of Jehovah's promises. Hebrews 11:13 observes that many of the faithful "died in faith, not having received the things promised, but seeing them from afar." This perspective teaches that faith's endurance is rooted in the certainty of God's Word, even when the timing of fulfillment remains future. Jehovah's promises are certain because He is incapable of falsehood, and His purpose is guided by perfect wisdom and love.

Jehovah's foreknowledge operates harmoniously with human free will. His omniscience does not mean He causes human decisions but that He perfectly knows how each moral agent will act in every possible circumstance. This understanding, known as middle knowledge, allows Jehovah to govern history without violating human freedom. His knowledge of future events resembles the way a barometer predicts the weather—it reveals what will occur without causing it. Therefore, while God foreknows the suffering and choices of humanity, He does not predetermine them; rather, He works within human history to bring about His ultimate purpose of redemption through Christ.

Faith that endures trusts this divine wisdom. It recognizes that Jehovah's purposes unfold across generations and that every promise will be fulfilled in its proper time. As 2 Peter 3:9 affirms, "Jehovah is not slow concerning His promise, as some people consider slowness, but is patient with you, not wanting anyone to be destroyed but all to attain to repentance." The faithful wait patiently for the coming of Christ's Kingdom, when sin, death, and suffering will be abolished. This hope sustains them through all imperfections of the present age.

To await Jehovah's fulfillment is not passive inactivity but active endurance rooted in faith, hope, and obedience. Christians continue to proclaim the good news, to strengthen one another, and to live by the moral standards of God's Word as they look forward to the day when His promises are realized fully. Their confidence rests in the assurance that "He who promised is faithful," and that every word He has spoken will come to pass in perfect righteousness.

Chapter 20 – The Ultimate Reward of Faith

Main Verse: 2 Timothy 4:7–8 – "I have fought the good fight, I have finished the course, I have kept the faith."

The Crown of Righteousness Promised to the Faithful

When the Apostle Paul wrote his final letter to Timothy, he stood at the threshold of death, not in despair, but in triumph. His confident declaration, "I have fought the good fight, I have finished the course, I have kept the faith," resounded as a testimony of a life wholly consecrated to Jehovah's service. The metaphor of the "good fight" evokes the image of a spiritual battle waged in loyalty to Christ. Paul's struggle was not against flesh and blood but against the spiritual forces of darkness (Ephesians 6:12). His perseverance was rooted in unwavering trust in Jehovah's promises through Christ Jesus.

Paul continues, "In the future there is reserved for me the crown of righteousness, which the Lord, the righteous Judge, will give to me on that day—and not to me only, but also to all who have loved His appearing" (2 Timothy 4:8). The "crown of righteousness" is not a mere token of victory, but the divine acknowledgment of a life vindicated by faith and perseverance. It signifies the believer's full acceptance before God through Christ, not by personal merit, but by grace through faith expressed in faithful obedience. This crown symbolizes the consummation of the believer's justification, when righteousness—now imputed by faith—will be imparted in fullness at the resurrection.

The use of "crown" (Greek: *stephanos*) reflects both the athlete's laurel wreath and the victor's eternal honor bestowed by the righteous Judge. Unlike earthly crowns that fade and decay, this crown is incorruptible (1 Corinthians 9:25). It is not earned by human effort but rewarded to those who have remained faithful to the end, maintaining trust in Jehovah and devotion to His Son. The faithful, like Paul, will be vindicated at the return of Christ, when He judges with perfect righteousness. Every act of endurance, every prayer uttered in faith, and every sacrifice made for the gospel will find its eternal recognition in that moment.

Faith's Completion in Resurrection Life

Faith reaches its ultimate fulfillment not in the temporal blessings of this life but in resurrection life. The Apostle Peter declared that believers are "protected by the power of God through faith for a salvation ready to be revealed in the last time" (1 Peter 1:5). Faith, in its truest form, does not end at death; it finds its completion when Jehovah restores life to the faithful through the resurrection.

The faithful Christian hopes not in this present age, which lies under Satan's influence (1 John 5:19), but in the age to come when death will be no more.

Paul speaks of this completion vividly in Philippians 3:10–11, desiring "to know Christ and the power of His resurrection." For him, the resurrection was not a vague hope but a concrete promise guaranteed by the resurrection of Christ Himself. Jesus is called "the firstfruits of those who have fallen asleep" (1 Corinthians 15:20), meaning that His resurrection assures the eventual resurrection of all who belong to Him. Faith's ultimate reward is therefore participation in that new creation, where mortality will be swallowed up by life (2 Corinthians 5:4).

For those chosen to rule with Christ in His heavenly Kingdom, the resurrection means transformation into incorruptible, immortal beings (1 Corinthians 15:50–53). For the rest of the faithful who inherit the earth, it means everlasting life in restored perfection under the reign of Christ and His co-rulers (Psalm 37:29; Revelation 21:3–4). Thus, the completion of faith is inseparably tied to the believer's resurrection destiny—whether heavenly or earthly—each according to Jehovah's purpose.

The Vindication of the Righteous

Throughout history, the righteous have often been misunderstood, persecuted, and maligned. Their faithfulness to Jehovah's truth has set them apart from a world that rejects divine authority. Yet Scripture assures that the faithful will ultimately be vindicated before all creation. Jesus Himself was vindicated in Spirit after being put to death in the flesh (1 Peter 3:18). Likewise, those who follow Him in faithfulness will share in His vindication when He returns.

The prophet Daniel foresaw this moment of vindication: "Many of those who sleep in the dust of the ground will awake, some to everlasting life, and others to reproaches and everlasting contempt" (Daniel 12:2). The resurrection thus serves as Jehovah's public declaration of who truly belongs to Him. Every false accusation, every injustice suffered for righteousness' sake, will be overturned. The world may have despised them, but Jehovah will honor them before angels and men.

Paul declares that God will "repay with affliction those who afflict you, and give relief to you who are afflicted" at the revelation of Jesus Christ (2 Thessalonians 1:6–7). This divine reversal is not a matter of human vengeance but of righteous judgment. The vindication of the faithful magnifies Jehovah's justice, proving that He rewards loyalty and condemns wickedness. Faith's endurance will then be fully justified as Jehovah's purpose unfolds before all creation.

The Final Judgment and the Reward of Believers

The ultimate reward of faith finds its culmination at the final judgment. The Scriptures describe a time when all humanity will stand before the judgment seat of Christ (Romans 14:10; 2 Corinthians 5:10). For the faithful, this is not a moment of terror, but one of confirmation and reward. Jesus declared, "The hour is coming when all who are in the memorial tombs will hear His voice and come out—those who did good things to a resurrection of life, and those who practiced vile things to a resurrection of judgment" (John 5:28–29).

This "resurrection of life" represents the full realization of redemption. Those who have kept the faith, like Paul, will be granted everlasting life as a gift from Jehovah through His Son (Romans

6:23). The judgment does not determine the believer's eternal destiny in uncertainty but reveals it publicly according to the righteous standard of Christ. It will demonstrate that faith, proven through obedience and endurance, has been genuine.

In contrast, the unrighteous—those who persist in rebellion and unbelief—will face eternal destruction in Gehenna (Matthew 10:28). The separation of the righteous and the wicked (Matthew 25:31–46) will manifest the moral perfection of Jehovah's judgment. Faith will then be rewarded with life, not as a wage earned, but as the promised inheritance of those who have remained steadfast under Christ's lordship.

The Eternal Kingdom of Christ

The eternal Kingdom of Christ is the sphere where the ultimate reward of faith is realized. This Kingdom, prophesied in Daniel 2:44, will crush and bring an end to all human kingdoms and stand forever. Jesus Christ, the appointed King by Jehovah, will rule with perfect justice and righteousness. Those who have endured faithfully will share in the blessings of this Kingdom, whether as co-rulers with Christ in heaven or as subjects of His righteous reign on earth.

For the heavenly rulers, Revelation 20:6 proclaims, "Blessed and holy is the one who shares in the first resurrection; over these the second death has no power, but they will be priests of God and of Christ, and they will reign with Him for a thousand years." These glorified ones will serve as Christ's associate kings and priests, administering His righteous rule. Their reward is not merely honor but participation in the divine plan to restore creation to perfection.

For the earthly faithful, the reward is everlasting life on a renewed earth, free from sin, suffering, and death (Revelation 21:3–5). Isaiah's vision of a paradise restored—where the wolf and lamb dwell together, and none harm or destroy (Isaiah 11:6–9)—will become reality. Faith, once tested in a world dominated by evil, will finally be rewarded with eternal peace under the rule of the Prince of Peace. Thus, the Kingdom represents the grand fulfillment of all God's promises through Christ, and the eternal home of all the righteous.

Everlasting Confidence in Jehovah's Faithfulness

The ultimate reward of faith is rooted not in human resolve, but in Jehovah's unwavering faithfulness. He cannot lie (Titus 1:2), and His promises are certain. The believer's confidence is therefore not self-generated but anchored in the reliability of God's Word. Throughout Scripture, Jehovah reveals Himself as the One who keeps covenant and steadfast love with those who love Him and keep His commandments (Deuteronomy 7:9).

Paul's confidence in facing death came from his assurance in Jehovah's trustworthiness. "The Lord will rescue me from every evil deed and will bring me safely to His heavenly Kingdom" (2 Timothy 4:18). That same confidence sustains all who remain faithful today. They know that their labor in the Lord is not in vain (1 Corinthians 15:58). Faith that endures to the end will never be disappointed, because it rests upon the eternal character of Jehovah Himself.

The faithful will not be forgotten. Their names are written in the book of life (Philippians 4:3; Revelation 3:5). Their hope is secure, their resurrection assured, and their inheritance preserved. Jehovah's faithfulness guarantees that every promise He has made will come to pass. As Paul wrote to the Thessalonians, "Faithful is He who calls you, and He also will bring it to pass" (1 Thessalonians 5:24). The ultimate reward of faith is therefore everlasting confidence—not merely in what believers receive, but in the unfailing goodness and reliability of Jehovah, who gives the reward.

Appendix A – Strengthening the Doubter

Main Verse: Mark 9:24 – "I do believe; help my unbelief."

Understanding the Weak in Faith

The confession found in Mark 9:24—"I do believe; help my unbelief"—captures the internal conflict common to many sincere followers of Christ. The father's cry before Jesus reveals both faith and frailty coexisting within the heart of a believer who desperately desires to trust but wrestles with weakness. This scene illustrates that doubt is not the absence of faith but the struggle of faith striving against uncertainty. Faith is not always perfect or complete; it must be cultivated through understanding, obedience, and continual reliance upon God's Word.

The Scriptures teach that all Christians are at different stages of maturity. Romans 14:1 urges believers to "welcome the one who is weak in faith, but not for disputes over opinions." The "weak in faith" refers not to unbelievers but to those whose understanding and confidence in God's promises are underdeveloped. They may waver when confronted with fear, temptation, or false teaching. Their uncertainty is not rebellion but spiritual immaturity. The Christian community must therefore respond with patient instruction and loving support rather than condemnation.

Faith develops by hearing and applying the Word of God (Romans 10:17). When believers neglect the Scriptures or fail to meditate upon them, their trust in Jehovah can falter. A weakened faith often stems from spiritual malnourishment, not hostility toward truth. Thus, the first step in strengthening the doubter is to restore that believer's connection to the living Word, for it is there that the Spirit-inspired message renews conviction, corrects misunderstanding, and strengthens the heart to persevere.

Abraham himself experienced moments of doubt before his faith was solidified. When Jehovah promised him descendants as numerous as the stars, Abraham asked, "O Sovereign Lord, how will I know that I will gain possession of it?" (Genesis 15:8). Yet God reaffirmed His covenant, and Abraham's faith grew stronger. Similarly, faith is often fortified through divine reassurance found in Scripture, where Jehovah's faithfulness is repeatedly proven across generations.

Restoring Confidence Through Scripture

The restoration of confidence for those weakened in faith must be rooted in Scripture, not in emotional reassurance or human reasoning. The Bible is not merely an ancient record but the living expression of Jehovah's will. Psalm 19:7 declares, "The law of Jehovah is perfect, restoring the soul; the testimony of Jehovah is sure, making wise the simple." It is through the divine message that the doubting heart is revived and the confused mind brought to clarity.

When Jesus confronted doubt, He directed individuals back to the written Word. After His resurrection, He said to the disciples on the road to Emmaus, "Was it not necessary for the Christ to suffer these things and to enter into His glory?" Then "beginning with Moses and all the Prophets, He interpreted to them the things concerning Himself in all the Scriptures" (Luke 24:26–27). Christ's example demonstrates that the cure for doubt is illumination through the Scriptures.

Faith must rest on truth, not sentiment. When the apostle Peter began to sink while walking toward Jesus on the water, it was not because he ceased believing that Christ existed, but because he allowed fear to outweigh trust (Matthew 14:30–31). Jesus did not rebuke him for his emotional struggle but for his "little faith." Peter's faith needed to grow in understanding of Christ's divine authority. Similarly, the believer who doubts must be led to know God more fully through His Word, for knowledge dispels uncertainty.

Regular study, meditation, and application of Scripture enable believers to confront false thoughts and worldly philosophies that undermine faith. Second Corinthians 10:5 teaches that we are to "bring every thought into captivity to the obedience of Christ." This intellectual discipline, guided by the inspired Word, transforms the mind, renews conviction, and restores assurance in God's promises.

The Role of Community and Shepherding

Jehovah designed the congregation as the environment in which faith matures and is sustained. Isolated believers are vulnerable to discouragement and doubt, while those integrated into a spiritual community benefit from mutual encouragement and accountability. Hebrews 10:24–25 commands believers to "consider how to stir up one another to love and good works, not neglecting to meet together." This communal life is essential to strengthening the weak and supporting those who struggle.

Christian shepherds—elders and mature overseers—are divinely appointed to guard, guide, and nurture the flock. Acts 20:28 instructs them, "Pay attention to yourselves and to all the flock, in which the Holy Spirit has made you overseers, to shepherd the congregation of God." Their role involves not merely administrative oversight but the spiritual care of souls in distress. A true shepherd imitates the Great Shepherd, Jesus Christ, who sought the wandering sheep and carried the weak with compassion (John 10:11).

For the doubter, personal fellowship and pastoral attention are indispensable. When one's faith is shaken, being reminded through counsel and prayer that he or she is not alone can provide critical strength. Galatians 6:1–2 exhorts believers to "restore such a one in a spirit of gentleness, keeping watch on yourself, lest you too be tempted. Bear one another's burdens, and so fulfill the law of Christ." This burden-bearing community is the antidote to isolation and despair.

Guiding with Patience and Compassion

Those who guide others through seasons of doubt must mirror the patience of Christ. The Lord never crushed the weak but strengthened them tenderly. Isaiah's prophecy of the Messiah states, "A bruised reed He will not break, and a dimly burning wick He will not extinguish" (Isaiah 42:3). This picture conveys His merciful approach to those barely holding on to faith.

The spiritually strong must recognize that doubt rarely disappears through debate or rebuke. Patience is essential. Second Timothy 2:24–25 instructs, "The Lord's servant must not be quarrelsome but kind to everyone, able to teach, patiently enduring evil, correcting his opponents with gentleness." The goal of patient correction is not to win an argument but to restore faith through truth and love.

Compassion must accompany patience. Jesus wept over Jerusalem's unbelief (Luke 19:41–42) and grieved when His disciples failed to trust Him during the storm (Mark 4:40). Yet His compassion did not excuse their weakness; it motivated Him to teach them more deeply. Shepherding the doubter means combining empathy with instruction—acknowledging emotional pain while leading the individual back to scriptural certainty.

Doubt thrives where compassion is absent. The fearful and the questioning often retreat when they sense judgment instead of care. Therefore, guiding with gentleness and understanding is not compromise; it is obedience to the example of Christ, who said to Thomas, "Do not be unbelieving, but believing" (John 20:27). Jesus met Thomas's weakness with evidence and grace, transforming his uncertainty into worship.

Prayer and Dependence on God's Wisdom

True strengthening of faith cannot occur apart from divine help. The father in Mark 9:24 understood this when he cried out, "Help my unbelief." Faith, though exercised by man, is sustained by God. James 1:5 teaches that if anyone lacks wisdom, he should ask God, who gives generously. Prayer is the believer's acknowledgment that his strength is insufficient and that spiritual endurance depends upon Jehovah's wisdom and guidance.

Prayer allows the doubter to approach God honestly, without pretense. The Psalms are filled with prayers of saints who struggled with fear, confusion, or discouragement. David, in moments of despair, prayed, "When I am afraid, I will put my trust in You" (Psalm 56:3). This is not the prayer of a man without faith but of one who battles inwardly to keep faith alive amid adversity. Jehovah answered such prayers with renewed assurance, proving that He does not despise humble confession.

For those who shepherd the doubter, prayer must also be central. It invites divine wisdom into counseling and discernment. The apostle Paul prayed for the believers in Ephesus that they might be "strengthened with power through His Spirit in the inner man" (Ephesians 3:16). Prayer, therefore, is both a personal and communal tool of restoration. It aligns human hearts with divine truth and empowers believers to persevere.

Dependence on God's wisdom means submitting to His timing as well. Strengthening faith is not an instant transformation but a process that unfolds through persistent trust, obedience, and reflection upon His Word. As the believer prays, studies, and applies Scripture, Jehovah gradually replaces uncertainty with assurance.

Turning Doubt into Steadfast Faith

Doubt, when addressed biblically, can become a catalyst for deeper faith. The same man who cried, "Help my unbelief," witnessed his son's miraculous healing and left with greater confidence in Christ's power. When believers bring their doubts honestly before God and submit them to His truth, He turns weakness into steadfast conviction.

James 1:2–4 exhorts Christians to "consider it all joy" when they encounter challenges, because "the testing of your faith produces endurance." While Satan exploits doubt to destroy faith, Jehovah uses it to strengthen believers who rely on Him. The process of overcoming doubt involves growth through Scripture, prayer, and fellowship. Each step forward deepens trust in God's character and Word.

Faith that has wrestled through uncertainty becomes resilient. The apostle Thomas, once a skeptic, became a bold witness, declaring, "My Lord and my God!" (John 20:28). His earlier doubts did not disqualify him but prepared him to proclaim the truth with conviction. In the same way, every believer who confronts and overcomes doubt through reliance on Jehovah's Word emerges stronger, humbler, and more compassionate toward others who struggle.

The aim of spiritual maturity is not to eradicate all questioning but to anchor one's trust unshakably in God's revelation. The believer learns that faith is not built upon human logic or emotional reassurance but upon the unwavering truth of Scripture. As Paul wrote, "Faith comes by hearing, and hearing by the word of Christ" (Romans 10:17).

To strengthen the doubter, therefore, is to guide him or her toward that living Word—where divine promises replace uncertainty, divine wisdom answers confusion, and divine love removes fear. The believer who once trembled before uncertainty can, through Scripture, prayer, and fellowship, stand firm in the confidence that Jehovah's Word is sure, His power sufficient, and His faithfulness unchanging.

Appendix B – How Can We No Longer Walk in the Futility of the Old Mind?

Main Verse: Ephesians 4:17 – "Now this I say and testify in the Lord, that you must no longer walk as the Gentiles do, in the futility of their minds."

Understanding the Futility of the Old Mind

The Apostle Paul's command in Ephesians 4:17–19 presents a profound call to transformation for all who belong to Christ. He writes, "So this I say, and affirm together with the Lord, that you walk no longer just as the Gentiles also walk, in the futility of their mind, being darkened in their understanding, excluded from the life of God because of the ignorance that is in them, because of the hardness of their heart; and they, having become callous, have given themselves over to sensuality for the practice of every kind of impurity with greediness." These verses reveal the spiritual anatomy of the unregenerate person and why a new life in Christ must reject the corruption and emptiness of that former state.

The "futility of their mind" describes a way of thinking that is devoid of true purpose and divine direction. The Greek term *mataiotēs* means "vanity," "emptiness," or "worthlessness." It refers to reasoning detached from the truth of God, a futile cycle of self-centered pursuits and moral blindness. This mindset characterizes those alienated from God, whose reasoning is corrupted by sin and darkened understanding. Such people may appear intelligent or accomplished in worldly matters, yet their minds are futile because they fail to recognize the Creator's authority, purpose, and moral standards.

Paul contrasts this futility with the renewal of the mind that accompanies salvation. The old way of thinking is based on deception, pride, and ignorance of God's truth. It leads to callousness, immorality, and greed. The new way of thinking, however, is based on the revealed truth of Christ, resulting in righteousness and holiness (Ephesians 4:22–24). Therefore, the believer must consciously abandon the mental habits of the old life and allow the truth of Scripture to shape new patterns of thought.

The Darkened Understanding and Exclusion from the Life of God

Paul's statement that unbelievers are "darkened in their understanding" shows the depth of spiritual blindness that sin causes. The human mind, apart from divine illumination, is incapable of perceiving spiritual reality. Romans 1:21 describes this same condition: "For even though they knew God, they did not honor Him as God or give thanks, but they became futile in their speculations, and their foolish heart was darkened." The heart of man becomes insensitive to the truth because sin obscures spiritual sight. This is not an intellectual problem but a moral and spiritual one.

The phrase "excluded from the life of God" underscores the tragedy of this condition. Alienation from God means separation from His presence, His moral light, and His sustaining power. The "life of God" refers not merely to biological existence but to spiritual life — fellowship with Jehovah, the source of truth and righteousness. Ignorance here is not mere lack of information but a willful rejection of divine revelation. People live in ignorance "because of the hardness of their heart." The Greek term *pōrōsis* refers to a kind of moral callus that renders a person insensitive to conviction and truth. When one continually resists God's will, the conscience becomes seared, as Paul also wrote in 1 Timothy 4:2.

This hardening leads to further corruption: "They, having become callous, have given themselves over to sensuality for the practice of every kind of impurity with greediness." Once the mind and heart are darkened, the person no longer responds to moral truth. This surrender to sin is self-inflicted — an abandonment of restraint and moral sensitivity. The phrase "given themselves over" indicates a voluntary act of rebellion. When a person chooses to live according to sensual desires, the conscience dulls, and the capacity for shame diminishes. Thus, walking in the futility of the mind is not only an intellectual problem but the result of an entire moral collapse.

The Transforming Power of the Renewed Mind

Against this dark background, Paul presents the transformative reality of the new life in Christ. In Ephesians 4:20–24, he writes, "But you did not learn Christ in this way, if indeed you have heard Him and have been taught in Him, just as truth is in Jesus, that, in reference to your former manner of life, you lay aside the old self, which is being corrupted in accordance with the lusts of deceit, and that you be renewed in the spirit of your mind, and put on the new self, which in the likeness of God has been created in righteousness and holiness of the truth."

The phrase "you did not learn Christ in this way" indicates that true discipleship is not merely acquiring information about Jesus but entering into a transformative relationship that renews the inner person. The believer "lays aside the old self," which refers to the entire corrupt nature inherited from Adam — the disposition inclined toward sin, self, and worldly thinking. This old self is "being corrupted" continually, demonstrating that sin never remains static but progressively destroys moral integrity.

To "be renewed in the spirit of your mind" means a continual process of transformation in the inner life, where motives, desires, and thought patterns are reoriented toward God. The "spirit of your mind" is not the Holy Spirit Himself but the human attitude and disposition shaped by truth under the Spirit's influence through Scripture. Renewal occurs as believers allow the inspired Word to reshape their reasoning, conscience, and affections. The new self, created "in the likeness of God," reflects His moral attributes — righteousness and holiness founded on truth.

The transformation is not mystical or emotional but rational and moral, grounded in divine revelation. Romans 12:2 reinforces this truth: "And do not be conformed to this world, but be transformed by the renewing of your mind, so that you may prove what the will of God is, that which is good and acceptable and perfect." The renewed mind discerns God's will and delights in obedience, whereas the old mind seeks self-gratification and independence from divine authority.

The Role of the Word of God in Renewing the Mind

The renewal of the mind is inseparable from immersion in the Scriptures. Jehovah has provided the inspired Word as the sole means of spiritual transformation. Hebrews 4:12 affirms that "the word of God is living and active and sharper than any two-edged sword," penetrating to the deepest parts of the human being and exposing motives and intentions. The believer must not depend on emotional experiences or human philosophy but on the objective truth revealed by God.

Jesus prayed to the Father, "Sanctify them in the truth; Your word is truth" (John 17:17). Sanctification — the process of being made holy — is achieved only through exposure to and obedience to divine truth. When a Christian meditates on the Word, he begins to think as God thinks. His perspective shifts from temporal to eternal, from selfish ambition to Christlike humility, from worldly values to heavenly priorities. Psalm 119:9–11 captures this principle beautifully: "How can a young man keep his way pure? By keeping it according to Your word. With all my heart I have sought You; do not let me wander from Your commandments. Your word I have treasured in my heart, that I may not sin against You."

The Spirit operates through the Word to renew the believer's inner life. There is no supernatural indwelling that bypasses Scripture; instead, the Holy Spirit's inspired revelation is the instrument through which God molds His people. The believer must study, meditate on, and apply Scripture daily, replacing the lies of the old self with the truths of God's character and promises. This consistent mental discipline gradually removes the futility of the old mind and replaces it with wisdom from above.

Putting Off the Old Self and Putting On the New

Paul uses the imagery of changing garments to describe the moral transformation that accompanies spiritual renewal. The believer is commanded to "lay aside the old self" and "put on the new self." This implies decisive action. The old patterns of deceit, greed, immorality, and anger must be intentionally discarded. Each sinful habit of thought and behavior belongs to the old life that died with Christ. Colossians 3:9–10 reiterates this truth: "Do not lie to one another, since you laid aside the old self with its evil practices, and have put on the new self who is being renewed to a true knowledge according to the image of the One who created him."

The "new self" is not a mere improvement of the old but a completely new creation in Christ. It is characterized by righteousness, holiness, and truth — the moral attributes of God Himself. As the believer grows in the knowledge of Scripture, his new nature expresses itself through attitudes and actions that reflect Christ's character. This includes humility, patience, compassion, and love for truth. The believer's moral transformation becomes visible evidence of the renewing work of the Word in his life.

Therefore, to "no longer walk in the futility of the old mind" means to live in daily submission to the truth of Scripture. The Christian must reject worldly philosophies, sinful desires, and selfish ambitions, embracing instead the righteousness and holiness that flow from a mind shaped by divine truth. The believer's thoughts, words, and deeds become aligned with God's revealed will, producing a life of purity and usefulness.

The Practical Outworking of a Renewed Mind

A renewed mind manifests itself in tangible obedience and spiritual discernment. Ephesians 4:25–32 provides concrete examples of how the renewed mind operates: speaking truth rather than falsehood, controlling anger, laboring honestly, using words to edify others, and forgiving as God in Christ forgave us. Each command represents a transformation from the old nature to the new. The mind renewed by Scripture understands that sin is not only offensive to God but destructive to the believer's witness and fellowship with Him.

The renewed mind also develops spiritual discernment, recognizing the deceptive allure of the world. First John 2:15–17 warns, "Do not love the world nor the things in the world. If anyone loves the world, the love of the Father is not in him." The old mind seeks pleasure, status, and independence, but the renewed mind values obedience, humility, and service. It measures success not by material gain but by faithfulness to God's will.

Moreover, a renewed mind cultivates gratitude and contentment. Philippians 4:8 instructs believers to think on what is true, honorable, right, pure, lovely, and praiseworthy. When a person directs his thoughts toward such things, he experiences peace that surpasses understanding (Philippians 4:7). The believer no longer lives as a slave to anxiety, lust, or pride because his reasoning is governed by the truth of God's Word.

Living in the Light of the New Mind

To live in the light of the new mind is to walk daily in fellowship with Jehovah through obedience to His Word. It is to think, reason, and act according to divine truth, rejecting the deceitful impulses of the flesh and the corrupt values of the world. The believer must continually examine his thought life, ensuring that it is saturated with Scripture and aligned with the will of God. Second Corinthians 10:5 calls believers to "take every thought captive to the obedience of Christ." This mental discipline protects the heart from drifting back into the futility of the old way of thinking.

This transformation is ongoing. The believer must "be renewed" continually, implying a lifelong process of sanctification. As long as the Christian remains in a fallen world, he must guard against the subtle influences of worldly reasoning and false doctrines. Therefore, the renewing of the mind requires perseverance, vigilance, and devotion to the truth. Through this ongoing renewal, the believer grows in spiritual maturity and conformity to Christ's likeness.

Appendix C – How Can We Deal with Spiritual Sicknesses of Mind and Heart?

Main Verse: Philippians 4:6-7 – "do not be anxious about anything, but in everything by prayer and supplication with thanksgiving let your requests be made known to God. And the peace of God, which surpasses all understanding, will guard your hearts and your minds in Christ Jesus."

Understanding the Nature of Spiritual Sickness

Spiritual sickness refers to the condition in which a person's thoughts, attitudes, desires, and emotions are misaligned with the will of Jehovah as revealed in His inspired Word. This sickness is not a mysterious, undefined malaise, but a real and definable deviation from the healthy spiritual condition that God desires for humanity. Just as physical illness results from an imbalance, infection, or breakdown in the body, spiritual sickness results from sin, worldliness, false teachings, demonic influence, or personal negligence in maintaining a right relationship with God.

Jeremiah lamented the deep spiritual sickness of Israel when he wrote, *"The heart is more deceitful than anything else and is desperately sick. Who can understand it?"* (Jeremiah 17:9, UASV). The Hebrew word translated "desperately sick" ('ānash) implies a terminal condition, indicating the depth of corruption that can exist within the human heart apart from divine intervention. Spiritual sickness leads to moral confusion, anxiety, depression, bitterness, pride, and a growing dullness to sin.

In the New Testament, Jesus addressed spiritual sickness by comparing His ministry to that of a physician: *"Those who are healthy do not need a physician, but those who are sick. I have not come to call the righteous, but sinners to repentance"* (Luke 5:31–32, UASV). Here, "sick" refers not to physical ailments, but to those who are spiritually lost and morally diseased.

Spiritual sickness affects both the mind and heart. The mind becomes clouded by false reasoning, deception, or worldly philosophies, while the heart—representing the seat of emotion and volition—is drawn away by fleshly desires and hardened against truth.

Identifying the Symptoms of Spiritual Sickness

Before one can treat spiritual sickness, it must be identified. This requires honest self-examination in the light of Scripture (Hebrews 4:12). Spiritual sickness may manifest in several ways:

Persistent Sin and Lack of Repentance

When a believer continually justifies or minimizes sin, it reveals a seared conscience (1 Timothy 4:2). Rather than confessing and forsaking sin, the spiritually sick individual tolerates it, eventually becoming enslaved to it (John 8:34).

Neglect of God's Word

A spiritually ill person may lack hunger for the Word of God. Jesus said, *"Man shall not live on bread alone, but on every word that comes from the mouth of God"* (Matthew 4:4, UASV). The absence of regular, meaningful intake of Scripture leaves the soul malnourished.

Prayerlessness

Communication with God is vital to spiritual health. When prayer becomes infrequent, shallow, or absent, the believer is spiritually anemic. Paul wrote, *"Pray without ceasing"* (1 Thessalonians 5:17), urging an ongoing, dependent relationship with Jehovah.

Bitterness, Envy, and Malice

Spiritual sickness often festers in relational sins. The apostle Peter urged believers to *"rid yourselves of all malice and all deceit and hypocrisy and envy and all slander"* (1 Peter 2:1, UASV). These poisons destroy love and unity within the body of Christ.

Doubt, Fear, and Anxiety

While trials may naturally evoke concern, ongoing anxiety and fear often stem from a lack of trust in Jehovah's sovereign care. Jesus warned against being "worried about your life" (Matthew 6:25), and

Paul exhorted believers to *"be anxious for nothing"* (Philippians 4:6), emphasizing a life anchored in God's peace.

Spiritual Apathy

A lukewarm spirit, as seen in the Laodicean congregation (Revelation 3:15–16), reflects a deeper sickness. The heart grows cold when the affections are diverted from God to the world.

Root Causes of Spiritual Sickness

Spiritual sickness does not emerge in a vacuum. Scripture identifies several root causes that must be addressed directly:

Sinful Flesh

The fallen nature of humanity is predisposed to rebellion against God (Romans 8:7). Paul describes this internal conflict: *"I find then the law that evil is present in me, the one who wants to do good"* (Romans 7:21, UASV). If not subdued by God's Word and Spirit-guided self-discipline, the flesh dominates.

Satanic Influence

Satan is called *"the god of this age [who] has blinded the minds of the unbelieving"* (2 Corinthians 4:4). He operates through lies, temptations, and false teachings to corrupt the mind and deceive the heart.

Worldly Influence

The world system, opposed to God, exerts constant pressure through media, entertainment, academia, and culture. The apostle John warned, *"Do not love the world nor the things in the world"* (1

John 2:15), because worldly attachments weaken spiritual convictions.

False Doctrine

Erroneous teachings distort God's truth and lead to spiritual ruin. Paul warned Timothy about those who *"will not put up with sound doctrine"* (2 Timothy 4:3). Only doctrinal clarity can guard the soul against the sickness of heresy.

Neglect of Spiritual Disciplines

Without regular intake of Scripture, prayer, fellowship, and service, the believer grows spiritually weak and vulnerable. Spiritual disciplines are not legalistic burdens but God-ordained means of grace and restoration.

God's Remedy for Spiritual Sickness

Jehovah, the Great Physician, offers a complete and sufficient cure for every form of spiritual sickness. His remedy includes both corrective and restorative measures rooted in the authority of Scripture.

The Healing Power of the Word

God's Word is essential for diagnosing and healing spiritual maladies. David testified, *"The law of Jehovah is perfect, restoring the soul"* (Psalm 19:7). The term "restoring" (Hebrew: *shub*) means to turn back or refresh. The Scriptures cleanse, convict, and correct (2 Timothy 3:16–17).

By regularly meditating on Scripture, the believer renews his mind (Romans 12:2) and regains spiritual clarity. The psalmist declared, *"Your word I have treasured in my heart, that I may not sin against you"* (Psalm 119:11). Memorization, study, and obedience to the Word are indispensable.

Genuine Repentance and Confession

Healing begins with sincere repentance. This involves turning from sin with godly sorrow (2 Corinthians 7:10). John assures believers, *"If we confess our sins, he is faithful and righteous to forgive us our sins and to cleanse us from all unrighteousness"* (1 John 1:9).

Confession is not merely verbal acknowledgment but heartfelt agreement with God's assessment of sin. It leads to realignment with His will and the restoration of spiritual vitality.

Persistent Prayer

James wrote, *"The effective prayer of a righteous man can accomplish much"* (James 5:16). Prayer reconnects the believer with Jehovah's power and presence. In moments of confusion, sorrow, or temptation, prayer becomes a lifeline.

David's many psalms of lament and repentance model how the spiritually sick can cry out for healing: *"Heal me, O Jehovah, for my bones are dismayed. And my soul is greatly dismayed"* (Psalm 6:2–3).

Fellowship and Accountability

Spiritual sickness thrives in isolation. Hebrews 10:25 warns against *"forsaking our own assembling together,"* because spiritual strength is cultivated through mutual encouragement and correction.

James 5:16 instructs believers to *"confess your sins to one another, and pray for one another so that you may be healed."* Christian fellowship provides a context for grace, restoration, and spiritual growth.

Holy Living and Obedience

Once a believer has been restored, obedience becomes both a fruit and a guard. Jesus said, *"If you love me, you will keep my commandments"* (John 14:15). Obedience nurtures a sensitive conscience, guards against relapse, and promotes joy.

Paul exhorted the Romans, *"Present your bodies a living and holy sacrifice, acceptable to God, which is your spiritual service of worship"* (Romans 12:1). This total consecration is the lifestyle of the spiritually healthy.

Encouragement for the Spiritually Sick

For those who feel weighed down by guilt, failure, or spiritual coldness, Jehovah offers real hope. He is "compassionate and gracious, slow to anger and abounding in loyal love" (Psalm 103:8). He heals not only the guilt of sin but the damage it causes in the soul.

Isaiah beautifully prophesied of the Messiah: *"He was pierced for our transgressions, He was crushed for our iniquities; the punishment for our peace was upon Him, and by His wounds we are healed"* (Isaiah 53:5). This healing includes reconciliation with God and the restoration of spiritual life.

No believer needs to remain in a spiritually sick state. The grace of God, the power of His Word, and the intercession of Christ (Hebrews 7:25) all work together for complete restoration.

Let every Christian pursue spiritual health with diligence. Paul wrote, *"Discipline yourself for the purpose of godliness"* (1 Timothy 4:7). Through consistent application of biblical principles and reliance on Jehovah's strength, every form of spiritual sickness can be overcome.

Bibliography

Andrews, E. (2018). *THE EARLY CHRISTIAN COPYISTS OF THE NEW TESTAMENT: The Making and Copying of the New Testament Books*. Cambridge: Christian Publishing House.

Andrews, E. (2020). *FROM SPOKEN WORDS TO SACRED TEXTS: Introduction-Intermediate New Testament Textual Studies*. Cambridge: Christian Publishing House.

Andrews, E. D. (2011). *AN INTRODUCTION TO BIBLE DIFFICULTIES So-Called Errors and Contradictions*. Cambridge: Christian Publishing House.

Andrews, E. D. (2012). *DIFFICULTIES IN THE BIBLE UPDATED: Updated and Expanded*. Cambridge, OH: Christian Publishing House.

Andrews, E. D. (2015). *CRISIS OF FAITH: Saving Those Who Doubt* . Cambridge, OH: Christian Publishing House.

Andrews, E. D. (2016). *HOMOSEXUALITY - THE BIBLE AND THE CHRISTIAN: Basic Bible Doctrines of the Christian Faith*. Cambridge, OH: Christian Publishing House.

Andrews, E. D. (2016). *INTERPRETING THE BIBLE: Introduction to Biblical Hermeneutics*. Cambridge, OH: Christian Publishing House.

Andrews, E. D. (2016). *THE BATTLE FOR THE CHRISTIAN MIND: Be Transformed by the Renewal of Your Mind*. Cambridge, OH: Christian Publishing House.

Andrews, E. D. (2016). *THE CHRISTIAN APOLOGIST: Always Being Prepared to Make a Defense [Second Edition]*. Cambridge, OH: Christian Publishing House.

Andrews, E. D. (2016). *THE COMPLETE GUIDE to BIBLE TRANSLATION: Bible Translation Choices and Translation Principles [Second Edition]* . Cambridge: Christian Publishing House.

Andrews, E. D. (2016). *THE EVANGELISM HANDBOOK: How All Christians Can Effectively Share God's Word in Their Community, [SECOND EDITION]*. Cambridge, OH: Christian Publishing House.

Andrews, E. D. (2017). *CONVERSATIONAL EVANGELISM: Defending the Faith, Reasoning from the Scriptures, Explaining and Proving, Instructing in Sound Doctrine, and Overturning False Reasoning [Second Edition]*. Cambridge, OH: Christian Publishing House.

Andrews, E. D. (2017). *DEFENDING OLD TESTAMENT AUTHORSHIP: The Word of God Is Authentic and True*. Cambridge, OH: Christian Publishing House.

Andrews, E. D. (2017). *EARLY CHRISTIANITY IN THE FIRST CENTURY: Jesus' Witnesses to the Ends of the Earth*. Cambridge, OH: Christian Publishing House.

Andrews, E. D. (2017). *HOW TO STUDY YOUR BIBLE: Rightly Handling the Word of God*. Cambridge, OH: Christian Publishing House.

Andrews, E. D. (2017). *IS THE QURAN THE WORD OF GOD?: Is Islam the One True Faith*. Cambridge, OH: Christian Publishing House.

Andrews, E. D. (2018). *CHRISTIAN APOLOGETIC EVANGELISM: Reaching Hearts with the Art of Persuasion.* Cambridge, OH: Christian Publishing House.

Andrews, E. D. (2018). *REASONING FROM THE SCRIPTURES: Sharing CHRIST as You Help Others to Learn about the Mighty works of God.* Cambridge, Ohio: Christian Publishing House.

Andrews, E. D. (2018). *REASONING WITH THE WORLD'S VARIOUS RELIGIONS: Examining and Evangelizing Other Faiths.* Cambridge, OH: Christian Publishing House.

Andrews, E. D. (2018). *The CHURCH CURE: Overcoming Church Problems.* Cambridge, OH: Christian Publishing House.

Andrews, E. D. (2019). *MIRACLES: What Does the Bible Really Teach?* Cambridge, OH: Christian Publishing House.

Andrews, E. D. (2019). *THE READING CULTURE OF EARLY CHRISTIANITY: The Production, Publication, Circulation, and Use of Books in the Early Christian Church.* Cambridge, OH: Christian Publishing House.

Andrews, E. D. (2020). *INERRANCY OF SCRIPTURE: How Can We Believe Inerrancy of Scripture In the Originals When We Don't Have the Originals?* Cambridge, OH: Christian Publishing House.

Andrews, E. D. (2022). *THE QUEST FOR THE HISTORICAL JESUS: Are Doubts About Jesus Justified?* Cambridge, OH: Christian Publishing House.

Andrews, E. D. (2023). *ARCHAEOLOGY & THE NEW TESTAMENT.* Cambridge, Ohio: Christian publishing House.

Andrews, E. D. (2023). *ARCHAEOLOGY & THE OLD TESTAMENT.* Cambridge, Ohio: Christian Publishing House.

Andrews, E. D. (2023). *BIBLICAL EXEGESIS: Biblical Criticism on Trial.* Cambridge, OH: Christian Publishing House.

Andrews, E. D. (2023). *CHRISTIAN APOLOGETICS: Answering the Tough Questions: Evidence and Reason in Defense of the Faith.* Cambridge, Ohio: Christian Publishing House.

Andrews, E. D. (2023). *HOW WE GOT THE BIBLE.* Cambridge, OH: Christian Publishing House.

Andrews, E. D. (2023). *ISLAM & THE QURAN: Examining the Quran & Islamic Teachings.* Cambridge, OH: Christian Publishing House.

Andrews, E. D. (2023). *ISLAMIC ESCHATOLOGY: Awaiting Al-Mahdi—The Twelfth Imam and the Future of Islam.* Cambridge, OH: Christian Publishing House.

Andrews, E. D. (2023). *JOHN CALVIN: A Solitary Quest for the Truth.* Cambridge, Ohio: Christian Publishing House.

Andrews, E. D. (2023). *THE BIBLE ON TRIAL: Examining the Evidence for Being Inspired, Inerrant, Authentic, and True.* Cambridge, Ohio: Christian Publishing House.

Andrews, E. D. (2023). *THE MACCABEES: The Hasmonaean Dynasty between Malachi and Matthew.* Cambridge, OH: Christian Publishing House.

Andrews, E. D. (2024). *BATTLE PLANS: A Game Plan for Answering Objections to the Christian Faith.* Cambridge, OH: Christian Publishing House.

Andrews, E. D. (2024). *CHRISTIAN APOLOGISTS OF THE SECOND CENTURY: Christian Defenders of the Faith.* Cambridge, OH: Christian Publishing House.

Andrews, E. D. (2024). *CHRISTIAN THEOLOGY: The Christian's Ultimate Guide to Learning from the Bible.* Cambridge, OH: Christian Publishing House.

Andrews, E. D. (2024). *CREATION AND COSMOS: A Journey Through Creation, Science, and the Origins of Life.* Cambridge, OH: Christian Publishing House.

Andrews, E. D. (2024). *DO WE STILL NEED A LITERAL BIBLE?: Discover the Truth about Literal Bibles.* Cambridge, OH: Christian Publishing House.

Andrews, E. D. (2024). *FAITH UNDER FIRE: Refuting the Top 30 Arguments Atheists Make Against Christianity.* Cambridge, OH: Christian Publishing House.

Andrews, E. D. (2024). *HELL: All You Need to Know About Hell.* Cambridge, OH: Christian Publishing House.

Andrews, E. D. (2024). *REASON MEETS FAITH: Addressing and Refuting Atheism's Challenges to Christianity.* Cambridge, OH: Christian Publishing House.

Andrews, E. D. (2024). *THE BABYLONIAN EMPIRE.* Cambridge, OH: Christian Publishing House.

Andrews, E. D. (2024). *THE BATTLE OF JERICHO—Myth or Fact?* Cambridge, OH: Christian Publishing House.

Andrews, E. D. (2024). *THE ENCYCLOPEDIA OF CHRISTIAN APOLOGETICS: The Resource for Pastors, Teachers, and Believers.* Cambridge: Christan Publishing House.

Andrews, E. D. (2024). *THE HISTORICAL ADAM & EVE: Reconciling Faith and Fact in Genesis.* Cambridge, OH: Christian Publishing House.

Andrews, E. D. (2024). *THE HISTORICAL JESUS: The Death, Burial, and Resurrection of Jesus Christ.* Cambridge, OH: Christian Publishing House.

Andrews, E. D. (2024). *UNDERSTANDING THE HITTITES: Biblical History, Archaeological Discoveries, and Etymological Clarifications.* Cambridge, OH: Christian Publishing House.

Andrews, E. D. (2025). *A FRESH LOOK AT PAUL'S THEOLOGY: Biblical Theology as Revealed through Paul.* Cambridge, OH: Christian Publishing House.

Andrews, E. D. (2025). *ATHEISM: What Will You Say to an Atheist.* Cambridge, OH: Christian Publishing House.

Andrews, E. D. (2025). *BIBLE DIFFICULTIES: How to Approach Difficulties In the Bible.* Cambridge, OH: Christian Publishing House.

Andrews, E. D. (2025). *BIBLICAL WORDS AND THEIR MEANING: An Introduction to Lexical Semantics.* Cambridge, OH: Christian Publishing House.

Andrews, E. D. (2025). *CAN WE TRUST THE BIBLE?* Cambridge, OH: Christian Publishing House.

Andrews, E. D. (2025). *DISCOVERING GENESIS ANSWERS: Exploring the Historical and Cultural Contexts of Genesis, One Insight at a Time (Answers from Genesis).* Cambridge, OH: Christian Publishing House.

Andrews, E. D. (2025). *DISCOVERING GENESIS ANSWERS: Tackling Tough Questions in Genesis: One Solution at a Time*

(Answers from Genesis). Cambridge, OH: Christian Publishing House.

Andrews, E. D. (2025). *DISCOVERING GENESIS ANSWERS: Unveiling the Truths of Creation, One Answer at a Time (Answers from Genesis).* Cambridge, OH: Chritian Publishing House.

Andrews, E. D. (2025). *EARLY CHRISTIANITY: Exploring Backgrounds, Historical Settings, and Cultures.* Cambridge, OH: Christian Publishing House.

Andrews, E. D. (2025). *IMMORTALITY OF THE SOUL: The Birth of the Doctrine.* Cambridge, OH: Christian Publishing Hiuse.

Andrews, E. D. (2025). *ISLAMIC IDEOLOGICAL JIHAD: Islamic-Funded, Islamic-Indoctrinated, Western Youth.* Cambridge, OH: Christian Publishing House.

Andrews, E. D. (2025). *JOSEPHUS & THE NEW TESTAMENT: Evidence from the First-Century Jewish Historian on Key Biblical Figures, Groups, and Events.* Cambridge, OH: Christian Publishng House.

Andrews, E. D. (2025). *LINGUISTICS AND THE BIBLICAL TEXT: Unlocking Scripture Through the Science of Language.* Cambridge, OH: Christian Publishing House.

Andrews, E. D. (2025). *OVERCOMING BIBLE DIFFICULTIES: Answers to the So-Called Errors and Contradictions [Second Edition].* Cambridge: Christian Publishing House.

Andrews, E. D. (2025). *PROVING GOD'S EXISTENCE.* Cambridge, OH: Christian Publishing House.

Andrews, E. D. (2025). *THE ANDREWS BIBLE BLUEPRINT: Unlocking Scripture's Truth, History, and Wisdom.* Cambridge, OH: Christian Publishing House.

Andrews, E. D. (2025). *THE ENCYCLOPEDIA OF THE TEXT OF THE NEW TESTAMENT: The Resource for Pastors, Teachers, and Believers.* Cambridge, OH: Christian Publishing House.

Andrews, E. D. (2025). *THE FACES OF ISLAM: Faith or Facade: Decoding Islam's Strategies.* Cambridge, OH: Christian Publishing House.

Andrews, E. D. (2025). *THE GUIDE TO SPIRITUAL WARFARE: Standing Firm in the Armor of God Against the Schemes of the Devil.* Cambridge, OH: Christian Publishing House.

Andrews, E. D. (2025). *THE STONES SPEAK: Biblical Archaeology and the Reliability of the Bible.* Cambridge, OH: Christian Publishing House.

Andrews, E. D. (2025). *WONDERFULLY MADE: Wonderful Are God's Works.* Cambridge, OH: Christian Publishing House.

Andrews, E. D. (2025). *YOUR YOUTH: The Young Christian's Guide to Making Right Choices.* Cambridge, OH: Christian Pubishing House.

Beattie, F. (2022). *CHRISTIAN APOLOGETICS [Annotated]: The Rational Vindication of Christianity.* Cambridge, OH: Christian Publishing House.

Kephart, E. B. (2022). *APOLOGETICS Annotated: A Treatise on Christian Evidences - [Annotated].* Cambridge, OH: Christian Publishing House.

REASONABLE FAITH

www.ingramcontent.com/pod-product-compliance
Lightning Source LLC
LaVergne TN
LVHW020930090426
835512LV00020B/3289